The North is a publication of
the poetry business
a workers cooperative

The magazine is published twice a year.
Edited by Ann Sansom and Peter Sansom. Reviews Editor: Holly Hopkins

Copyright © 2025 The Contributors
All Rights Reserved
ISSN 0269-9885
ISBN 978-1-914914-84-3

Designed & typeset by Utter Design utter.co.uk.
Cover image: from the cover of *The Tightrope Wedding* by Michael Laskey.
Printed by Page Bros.

No part of this publication may be reproduced without the consent of the publishers.

We are currently only considering work submitted online (not by post). Please go to www.poetrybusiness.co.uk/about/submissions/ for more details.

We are grateful for the financial assistance of Arts Council England.

Distributed by BookSource, 50 Cambuslang Road, Cambuslang Investment Park, Glasgow G32 8NB.

Advertising rates on request.

Subscribe to *The North*

Current rate is £22 per annum or £44 for two years (digital version £16/£22), single copies £12 (digital version £9) (overseas print subscription £28 per annum or £56 for two years, single copies £14).

Subscription address:
The Poetry Business,
Campo House, 54 Campo Lane
Sheffield S1 2EG tel 0114 4384074.
www.poetrybusiness.co.uk/product-category/the-north/subscriptions/

Correspondence address:
email: office@poetrybusiness.co.uk

Please make cheques etc. payable to The Poetry Business

www.poetrybusiness.co.uk

N71 POETRY

154 POEMS BY 83 POETS

Isobel Dixon
David Constantine
David Tait
James Bradley
Niamh Twomey
Jackie Wills
Penelope Shuttle
Roy Marshall
Brendan Cleary
Philip Rush
Martin Hayden
Jenny McRobert
Martyn Crucefix
Ramona Herdman
Howard Wright
Lauren Camp
John Lynch
June Crebbin
Elizabeth Chadwick
Pauline Plummer
Jacci Bulman
John Goodby
Orlagh O'Farrell
Maitreyabandhu
Tim Dooley
Sue Riley
Julie Lumsden
Lorraine Mc Ardle
Ian Pople
Maggie Reed

Nia Broomhall
Jean Stevens
Fokkina McDonnell
Barbara Marsh
Terry Quinn
Paul Mills
David Underdown
Meg Cox
Mike Di Placido
John Lancaster
Stephen Payne
Pam Thompson
Robert Etty
Robert Hamberger
Vasiliki Albedo
Christy Ku
Liz Byrne
Charlotte Wetton
Rod Whitworth
Mary Noonan
Siún Carden
Michael Henry
Lydia Harris
Jenny King
Jon Miller
Ben Maguire
Jim McElroy
Amy Dugmore
Eilis Stanley
Rosie Hadden

Jeanette Burton
Lydia Macpherson
Graham Mort
Rebecca Althaus
Cliff Yates
Linda Ford
Angela Neenan
Marion New
Matthew Paul
Michael Laskey
Jayant Kashyap
Cia mangat
Zelda Cahill-Patten
Charlie Jolley
Caroline Bracken
Jen Feroze
Dale Booton
Kate Rutter
James Appleby
Ger Duffy
Derval Tubridy
Nigel Pantling
Dean Parkin

**For A Full List Of Poems
Please See Back Pages**

N71 PROSE

FOCUS FEATURE

Michael Laskey at Eighty 72
Anne Berkeley, Liz Berry, Peter Carpenter, Helen Ivory, Naomi Jaffa, Hannah Lowe, Kath Mckay, Ian McMillan, Helena Nelson, Naomi Shihab Nye, Dean Parkin, Stephen Payne, Sheenagh Pugh, Christopher Reid, Philip Rush, Jacqueline Saphra, Paul Stephenson, Alicia Stubbersfield, Emily Wills, Anthony Wilson and **Tamar Yoseloff**

FEATURES

Poets I Go Back To 68
Jane Draycott and **Kate Potts**

Featured Title 108
From Secrets Corner, Dean Parkin, The Garlic Press

Blind Criticism 110
Anna Hiller, **Rishi Dastidar** and **Ed Reiss** on 'Bomber'

PUBLICATIONS

New Poets Prize 2024 Winners and Runners Up 88

International Book & Pamphlet Competition 2024 Winners, Runners Up and Commended 96

Nigel Pantling
A Foreign Country 104

REVIEWS

Sarah-Clare Conlon 115
on Lisa Robertson, Anthony Vahni Capildeo, Janette Ayachi

Lydia Unsworth 119
on Martina Evans, Katy Evans-Bush, Tim Tim Cheng

Lenni Sanders 122
on Tom Jenks, Harry Man, Kandace Siobhan

Ian Pople 125
on Elisa Gonzalez, Victoria Chang, Carlie Hoffman

Edmund Prestwich 128
on Sasha Dugdale, Imtiaz Dharker, Michelene Wandor

Belinda Cooke 131
on Marie Howe, Grace Wilentz

Sally Baker 134
on Amanda Dalton, Rebecca Watts, Victoria Gatehouse

Kayleigh Jayshree 137
on Amelia Loulli, Lucy Mercer, Emily Berry

the PB

Recent titles from smith|doorstop

Spin **by Laurie Bolger**
Winner of the 2023 International
Book & Pamphlet Competition
Published March 2024

A Coalition of Cheetahs **by Doreen Gurrey**
Winner of the 2023 International
Book & Pamphlet Competition
Published March 2024

Mahogany Eve **by Alan Payne**
Published May 2024

Five
Poems by Eva Lewis, Helen Bowell,
Laura Potts, Prerana Kumar, Ruth Yates
Published July 2024
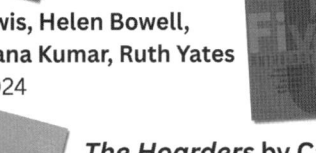

The Hoarders **by Caleb Leow**
Winner of the 2023 New Poets Prize
Published August 2024

All Appears Ordinary **by Freya Bantiff**
Winner of the 2023 New Poets Prize
Published August 2024

The Naming of Names **by Shash Trevett**
Published August 2024

The Luck **by Jane Routh**
Published October 2024

COAL: Poems, Prose, Photographs
Edited by Sarah Wimbush, Ann Sansom
and Peter Sansom
Published November 2024

A Dress with Deep Pockets **by Jen Feroze**
Winner of the 2024 International
Book & Pamphlet Competition
Published March 2025

Boy, Mother **by Caroline Bracken**
Winner of the 2024 International
Book & Pamphlet Competition
Published March 2025

A Foreign Country **by Nigel Pantling**
Published April 2025

available at www.poetrybusiness.co.uk

ISOBEL DIXON

Thoughts on the 22:20 Avanti West Coast Train to London Euston

You're not home anymore, Lancaster.
The pharmacy I took the morning after
in has shut, moved streets and changed
its name, a stab to my womb, like I didn't
fall in love here at least twice over.

And no one wants to be that person,
the one who can't just leave it all behind.
Dad constantly reminisces about his attic
room and his flat mate, Neil, who microwaved
frozen pizzas for dinner every night. I get it
now, how for the rest of my life I'll smile about

sex poems read in 9ams and the smell of re-
renewed library books, the hot chocolates,
the vapes, the nights out in the snow, sheer
tops, red bras, no jackets, skin raw, 8pm netball
matches, Jane Austen lectures, pints for £2.50
on Wednesdays, watching The Chase with my
housemate, ritualised, embedded, imprinted.

I came back to see my friends and drink wine.
It was November, and that fleetingly visiting
Ferris wheel stared me right in the face. The red
man at the traffic lights mocked me, letting it loom.
A full circle moment; first kissed the boy I didn't even
like at the top of it, how pathetically straight. But I laugh
about it now, all those bus rides I spent willing God
to grant me a girlfriend, and then I bedded a boy instead.

When he was in my house that December, I asked
him to spot the condom amongst the balloons on
our living room floor. We'd blown them up for Laura's
birthday in October. Kept them because they weren't
deflating on their own. Popping them at the end of the
year was no better than a funeral, the pile of ruptured
plastic lifeless and tacky, ready to meet the alleyway bin.
To join them was tempting. So was hiding in the walls
of our contract-expired home, to linger there a little longer.

DAVID CONSTANTINE

Transit of the bin-men

Lucky you if you were present that late afternoon
At the leisure hour on that particular street
Which is a narrow canyon, long and high, its pavements swilled

To overflowing with drinkers, idlers, buyers and sellers, watchers
Lucky you if you were there at the happy-hour conjunction
Of light, the light, slanting in low and exactly

When the bin-lorry made its entrance, the operatives
The menials out of Africa, riding behind, each on an iron plate
In the stink and din either side the maw. It was them

Above all others and above all else the slant light showed
In their luminescent green and flashed-with-silver gear
Those timed men day by day clocked in and out

How they rode the interludes with utter nonchalance
Till the halt and the leaping down for the next crammed bins, so deft
Their fitting these in the grips that lift and tilt and empty

What must be got shut of. And leapt up then and rode on casually
Like lords at ease. Don't say the last daylight angling in like that
Only gilded them – ah no, it showed

What innermost they were, their quickness, skill and gaiety
In each that light brought out
The dancer and all the spectacle, the theatre, the performance

They had in them to offer. So with slow haste
In stops and starts, speediness and lounging
They forced their loud and necessary passage through an audience. Meanwhile

The topmost rooms attract the slanting glances of the last of that day's sun
The watered red geraniums in their window-boxes thrive
And screaming swifts criss-cross the immaculate blue.

Lifeline

That late autumn, a year to the day, her grief
Became demanding. She rose very early
Opened the bedroom window an inch or two
And sat in the dark at a small table
Her hands round a mug of coffee. She heard
The slop of the tide with the breeze behind it
And she watched and not for daybreak but for
A lamp to be lit atop the mainmast
Of the one and only fishing boat out there.

So she before dawn sat watching and waiting
In what some have called the sure and certain hope
Till from the swaying mast, rapid, undulant
Like a narrow carpet from a blank elsewhere
On the backs of the waves, the light, a lifeline
Was flung to her, to be a hold of sorts
Briefly tethering the vast out-there to home.
A while she held its quick life with her eyes.

Then it was done. Her magic carpet vanished.
She watched the teetering light diminish
Down the sound into the bleak Atlantic.

Some such mornings she drank up her coffee
And went back to bed. Others, the better ones
She would bide quiet, warming the empty mug
Between her hands. She watched the daylight in
She watched for two, harbouring in her his love
For their small island's brave reappearance
Under the encouraging or the baleful skies.

Aurelia in hiding

My consultant has long and very beautiful fingers.
Look there, she said, pointing the middle at the image on the screen
It is the aurelia biding her time in your *arbor vitae*

The first I've seen in that place and I doubt I'll see another.
I asked would my visitant stay to the bitter end?
Most don't, she answered. All depends how alive you are

In that branching and leafing of the brain, what encouragement
And quiet you can offer her. She is in hiding
She is preparing a revelation, she will be beautiful, she wants

A progeny, she'll flit if you make her nervous. I asked
Would I feel her leave? Some do, some don't, she answered.
I'm no expert, but you seem to me one who will

And whether or not her departure has your blessing
Rests with you, what sort of a host you were, what harbouring
You gave that golden migrant in your tree of life.

Speech Day

He came on last, when his colleagues, the Heads of Year
Had spoken the names and shaken the hands and given the prizes
He, the High Master, back stage, hearing the bouts of applause

Quietly collecting himself, biding his time
Wearing as ever his old university's gown and hood
Entered at last, as he always had, a respectful total silence

Halted front stage and as always without a script
Stood smiling. He who, year upon year on the same occasion
Always with some new slant, new emphases, a new joke or two

Had spoken the expected praise and encouragement
Always at ease, always sure of the fund of words in him
Stood now where he had always stood before the lifted faces

With their thousand eyes on him he stood and they
    watched and waited
And in a lengthening silence saw a man's mouth opening
    and closing
Like that of a goldfish in a bowl and no sound came out

There was no voicing, there were no words but a man stood
Mechanically opening and closing his mouth
And could make not even the shape of one solitary dumb syllable

And showed to his audience the face of unspeakable terror.

DAVID TAIT

Faerie

You told us you'd just seen a faerie,
and when we asked you showed us the place,
saw it stranded there in the grass.

Sometimes faeries have a need to be lifted,
for their wings to catch in light breeze.
How lucky then that this one caught your eye.

You lift them and they fly, and walking back
you're happy to have been helpful, and tell your dad
who says it was a good kind thing.

You're too young yet to be told of seeds and weeds,
and after all, don't *thistledown* and *sugar-stealer*
sound a little like fae names?

Later we walk around Fountains Abbey,
and the air is bristling with fairies.
We've become much too old to see them,

when they fly up to our eyes
we brush them away.

Leighton Moss

Someone has carved a tree bough
into the shape of an owl

on the walk between viewing posts,
my feet clanking on the wooden planks.

All the hides are named after birders
but I don't remember their names.

I'm new to this. I don't have binoculars,
but I do carry sorrow between each wooden hut,

I do carry my need to be alone and away.
There are marsh harriers and bitterns

somewhere in the reeds, and if you listen,
the distinctive call of bearded tits,

some of whom are showing off their latest gear.
Ospreys don't live here but they visit the shallows.

One arrives, the call goes up and everyone jerks
to watch it. A boy lends me his glasses

and I see it, a golden scimitar with a white breast
arrowing down towards the reeds, the collective catch

of breath and joy, the sigh of those who've got
what they came for, even if they can't say why.

I talk to a man who woke at 5am to drive here
from the Midlands. *It's the birds and the people*

he says, *and to see something like that, well,
I wouldn't miss it for a dozen worlds.*

JAMES BRADLEY

Between Storms

Shropshire rain and then the sun
the buzzards circling above the woods,
I walk towards the road, past a field
of yellow flowers, sheep drowsing
in the shadow of an oak.

The silence here is careless and malleable,
like a guard who's drifted off at his post.
Let him sleep, let him drape his arm
over his lover. Don't write him up.
It isn't down to him if we'll be saved.

Hoopoe

in the Hai Dian district
flitting matter-of-factly
as you grace the bare branches
of a grim Beijing winter
your burning ochre flicker
upends all regularity.
In my native realistic city
of rain-sodden starlings
I pored for a decade over
your frozen illustration
in *The Book of British Birds*
your crown a bristling quiff
a sunburnt savannah headdress
a fantastic feathered Elvis
among the monochrome austerity
of stern Atlantic seabirds
but the sober maps informed me
that you alighted only rarely
onto privileged spots of orange
on unthinkable English coasts.
Now we're both a long way
from where we should be.
How odd to see you here, bright
stranger; much smaller and more
beautiful than I wished for.

NIAMH TWOMEY

Herb

Noun. Like *weed* or *love*, a human construct.
A category for a plant whose stem remains
soft as a limb, never hardens to wood like *tree*.
Whose leaves/stems/flowers are used
for food or medicine. Here is the human again,
over-filling his pockets with parts of you, leaving
in return a word. Like *loss*. Like *perennial, native, harvest*.
Usefulness, another of the invention he blesses you with.
And look, he has drawn you all with one green pencil and labelled
Rosemary. Calendula. Marjoram. Parsley. Yarrow
for his records, definitive proof that you exist.

Follow Me

Back then my Dad would have followed me to the moon,
parked up beside it and read the paper while he waited.

His car lurked where nightclubs coughed me up
and friends asked ...*is that your dad?*
       Aren't you coming home with us?

He waited outside each window I was pressed up against
while some boy unzipped me,

pumped his cock through my lockjaw.
I hated him for it.

Tonight, walking home under a bruised moon,
only my own footsteps tut-tutting,

I remember the crossword flung on the dash,
swallowed rage, a look that said
you're better than all of this.

JACKIE WILLS

At Arrivals

You walk past cardboard signs,
strangers' names held up like trophies.
Your suitcase is heavy with river water.
You drag it from the conveyor belt, spinning
like a compass. From here on life is tidal.
Friendships ebb and flow. Home
is a sailboat rocking on the horizon.
No one in this airport – in this world –
will wipe the salt from your skin.

The Night Before I Turn 70

Sixty-nine ticks off its minutes. The cat feels it,
pawing me as I prepare to demolish my desk,
toolbox heavy on the stairs as water lugged uphill.

That evening before my son was ten the curve
of nine was so roundly human it sat listening
to a story. I don't want to be ten, he said.

It was fine, June was hot, we ate ice-cream.
I'm turning in mid-winter. It's a night for destruction.
I lever nails, unscrew dusty heads, ease off the frame.

My desk donates a pair of cabinets to the bed.
They stand on either side, relatives at a wake,
shelves, top, exterior panels, unsure of what to do

but mourn. The base remembers being a washstand
in another century and they're reminiscing
about bodies bowing towards a bowl of water,

rubbing soap into suds. They've half forgotten skin
and its vanities. The scrape of a razor, a cut. Planets
shum like a chorus of women whose job is to explain.

PENELOPE SHUTTLE

hip hip hooray

in a Malvern mist the sun adopts the coif for distinction's sake
the sun is a silent postcard
the sun is a bell-chant in a blue dungeon of air

the sun says, the bible is the wrong book
the sun says, I will quench the angels, rubric by rubric
the sun says, I will make a mock-charter with the stars

the sun is watching the old moon felled by Jupiter
the sun is busy as a sheep fair
the sun is the high hood of the mountains

the sun says, the ruins of the convent must include a wishing well
the sun allows the moon some of his light
but never at the point of noon

the land bridges of the sun are all burnished as if for sale
the sun is organizing bush fires and barbeques
the sun wears a candle flame for a brooch

the sun is a rose cult
the sun is setting fire to himself
the sun is a celebrity shrine

recalls with a smile
the excessive autumn rains of 1369
and how he could have sent a fox a love letter   but did not

Arwyn Place
28 January 2025

whenever I sit down
to rest
from my labours
with laundry
office or garden
the dead gather round me
asking to be remembered
it is quiet now
they say
we can talk   no-one
will overhear   or interrupt us

    but it is hard to bear
    their hearts are so full
    and so   is mine

ROY MARSHALL

Lull

A rutted track bisected woods
and led up to a three-bar gate
that opened onto frosted fields.
How weird, to see a hare approach
and lope to a halt, a leap from us.
My dog raised her paw but didn't
give chase, as if this were some Eden
where creatures came without fear
to share the rhythm of their hearts
in peace. We stood a while in clouds
of breath, close as those soldiers
in no-man's land at Christmas, until
the hare broke the spell and headed,
without urgency, back up the hill.

A Fire

We dropped our bikes
at the field edge,
made a solemn circle
of stones and bricks,
assembled a pyre
of dried grass and twigs.
The match, lit and lowered.
Flame licked a page
of newsprint, sent smoke
to dance on the wind,
as if our very own genie
rose before us, our only wish
already granted by this
pristine fire.

The air shimmered,
two faces flushed
with heat, miles from shops
and streets, the sticky tar
of roads, the tinny spillage
of radios, the only sounds
a blackbird's call,
and the crack and hiss
of sticks. All adults
extinct, for all we knew,
and all our days
of boredom, punishment,
restraint, going up
into the blue.

BRENDAN CLEARY

Reservoir

too still
for comfort

we find ourselves
here before dusk

vapours stronger
from our past

so haunted
we'll stay

gaze at each other
fearful & lost

a sky too vast
the water approaching

Classics

wrecked in the head
waking in doorways

he said the birdsong
reminded him of Stravinksy

The Rite of Spring
& it couldn't be sustained

of course not
no way Renee!

so you left him
you had to

left him to rot
reflect in afterglow

the Mozart tattoo
above his left elbow

PHILIP RUSH

Solidarity and Peace

A Kind of Epitaph for Peter Sinfield (1943-2024)
'The fate of all mankind I fear is in the hands of fools.'

It was a demonstration against war,
against genocide in Gaza, against
the bombing of Lebanon, and Ken Loach spoke
firm and clear, of solidarity and peace.
In every one of his films the kestrel dies.
There's surely a scene where a couple scours
the Ten Commandments from the masonry
of a quiet parish church. Down with thou shalt nots
and long live love, the blessed and the happy!
The helpless, the landless and the poor,
the disfigured and the marginalised,
the whole gang of Beatitudes,
they are the stars in Ken Loach's films.
That must be the one with the vicar actually interrupting
the shoot to complain about the theology
and then Loach leaving that whole scene in
as if it had been as tightly scripted as the opening
where a woman in a scruffy teeshirt wears
the look of a saint. Great cinema.
'The wall on which the prophets wrote,'
Peter said, 'is cracking at the seams.'
Melodrama, someone told me once,
starts with a social problem which bugs us all,
eg the treatment of workers & the enormous wealth
of the mill owner. Then the mill-owner's daughter
gets off with the union man's lad. Naturally.
The lovers meet beside mill streams
or in the back rooms of noisy pubs.
When they announce their engagement,
the play can end and the audience has been
fooled into thinking that a huge political debate
has been resolved. The image of a kestrel
soars into clear sky. Like Ben says in his book,
'The song goes on forever then stops.'
Okay, maybe not a novelist, a war photographer,
the film closing as she receives a barrage
of honest applause at a prize gala.
Another thing about melodrama is documents.
Letters, records, and pieces of paper.
Inheritance, identity, permissions to remain.
Enter a spruce junior officer with a sheet of A4:
'You need to see this, ma'am.'
It's a crime series and the signal social issue
is racial stereotyping and prejudice.
In the end, the bodies having piled up
and the evil police chief now under arrest,
Inspector Suave brings a bottle
of pricey wine to ma'am's flat
where she's combed out her hair.
They dine intimately on a dimly lit set.
There's forgiveness, there's forgetting,
there's red wine swilling thickly in a raised glass,
and there's a kestrel which always dies.

MARTIN HAYDEN

An incomplete, unrhymed sonnet, in memory of Peter Abbs, poet and educationalist

In a Sheffield dusk, on a hillside
above the city, after a poetry seminar
I was enthusing about *The Making
Of the English Working Class* which he hadn't
found time to read, though it was on his (long)
list, and I kept quiet about being only
half-way. With baffled pleasure he explained
how he was under attack from a now
'stunningly beautiful' activist daughter,
blamed for the world as it was, her reply
to his 'All my work is trying to change it!'
'You're not doing it fast enough.'

JENNY McROBERT

First Gooseberry

You won't find them in Tesco or Aldi, no one
likes sickly green with white veins running through,
like dismembered eyeballs or jellyfish tentacles. No one
likes the hairy bit on the top...or bottom? No one
likes the idea of being surplus to requirements, the one
stuck in the middle and yet
that first taste from bush to mouth
was a glory of little seasons
on the tongue, a lesson
in staying power, a hoping
that one of them will come through
like a sweetmeat, like
a small beginning
pressed-juicy between
your thumb and forefinger waking
hot in your mouth.

MARTYN CRUCEFIX

Scream
the collective noun for swifts

In a terraced cottage named after the small birds
  that flew round the eaves; the languid beauties
of John William Waterhouse hang on the walls;
  scrambled eggs for breakfast in the cold basement;
stare across the valley while you stand to shave,
  a radio on the windowsill: high registers always
for the ranks of the angels. Silk once was woven
  beyond the church spire, driven by the confluence
of streams off the hills. The water's power's gone,
  laid off, the workers who'd wake to the ceiling
you woke to this morning. The mills turned to flax,
  to flour, to cider, trade killed by foreign wars.
A choir in the church: you explore the narrow lanes,
  planning a tour of the world's settled places, yet
first, taking stock, in a cottage named for those birds:
  for more than a century they nested in the eaves.

Things Newborn

You can almost see the crisp cellophane
        from the shop still round them: red-streaked
carnations in a vase, on a desk, for our arrival;
      beneath the traffic at Wadebridge, a glint
          of the crooked river (the Camel), making

its way to the sea at Stepper Point; last night,
      on the next table, a family of five (or was
one the invited boyfriend?), mother and father
      worn thin, the teens bright and nervy at such
          an enforced, strange occasion, to be faced

without phones; the flowers are a nice touch,
     in truth, they focus, a magnet for the filings
of mind, of scattered memory, some lines
     from *The Winter's Tale*; after a journey,
         conversation grows stilted, even awkward.

Then pick up a pen. After a long drive, orientation
      is difficult: staring from windows
at the river, across the ring road, a Travelodge
      this way, a neighbour's untidy garden the other;
         then, as if from an unpromising, forced bud,

waking, a bloom, a way of expressing things
     like catching sight of one of the teenagers,
no, two of them, phones cradled in their laps,
     under napkins, hidden below the lip
        of the formal table, sly, their energies earthed.

RAMONA HERDMAN

Every medical appointment is like a job interview

> *My efforts began to feel like an unconvincing charade, one in which I played the roles of both the charlatan and his mark.*
> – Mike Mariani *A catalogue of losses: what chronic fatigue syndrome took away from my life*

I try to be both factually correct and compelling.
I try to provide concrete examples that people
can understand and believe in two to three minutes.

I structure my answers: Situation, Target, Action, Results.
I have lists prepared of strengths (not too unlikely)
and weaknesses (not too troublesome or trifling).

I try to be likeable and also *Don't fuck with me.*
I make the most of being a middle-class professional.
I help them imagine I'd Fit In With The Culture Here.

I dress for the position. Would the person they want
brush her hair? How smart is too smart? I lie fluently,
as always, when they ask why I want the job.

Conditional

Last week I thought
if only my eyes didn't hurt
I'd be happy.
Now look at me –

without that top note of pain
all my other complaints
raise their voices to howl
like cats in a barrel.

Lemons

After 'The Orange' by Wendy Cope

Another day sunk in my duvet –
I've done none of the things on my list
except try and hope to get better.
Without doing, how do I exist?

HOWARD WRIGHT

Promise

They can cast their hooks –
a shimmering net of sharps –
out towards me

but the boats are so small,
their movements unpredictable
and the fog hazes everything.

So they can think afterwards
they've got me
but I can be anywhere,

meeting their gaze
with a face open as the sun off the sea,
an eye wet and clear

as one anonymous silver darling
turning and gleaming
like a knife in the deeps.

Transfigured
Schoenberg

The vaulted hall decorated
with closed windows and whispers,
poetry recited high in the gods
over Echo's scattered bones,
the stage and acoustics spotlight
teenage girls in split black dresses
for ballroom or romance, the bald
conductor as if he owns the place;
the orchestra, his young orchestra
smiling at his turned back, their tone
filling the void with discordance,
dissonance, duplications of smile
and shoulder, mirror of leg,
signalling they clearly hear and see
the world as this music, as one.

LAUREN CAMP

One to Borrow Trouble

Oryx or antelope move
in open fields. Oryx in a loop and the juniper
titmouse with their triplicate rhythms.

A train occupies the plain, boxcars and tanks conferring.

A wire keeps braying.

I remember thinking
the election is past.
Expressed as I mistook it for
the deepest work but it was
not even that.
In the morning, I find a snake on the porch.

Drop Me to My Knees

The day is always a small bit of truth and many easy griefs.

Homeless wait on the near corner with signs: *Want to buy a tent*, or *Have you ever felt invisible*.

History moves on through
shifting registers and size.

Vinny draws tilting eagles.

We know the dual need to praise every unsettling curse.

The woman who plays washboard in bluegrass bands on Saturdays sighs and says *It's like an amen again and again* and

I scribble that down in smeared blue.

JOHN LYNCH

Antarctica

I look at Keith's face for a long time,
before reading about the road conditions
that night, how the lorry and motorcycle
just slid, that he was riding pillion, then

I'm with him again: Miss Van der Graaf's
let him bring his sledge in because it's finally
snowed, and those of us with coats and wellies
trudge all the way across the football pitch

to the centre spot, which is the South Pole,
and stick our Union Jack in the ground.
Then, she tells us about Amundsen,
the return journey, and the little tent at the end.

After school, the snow is hard and shiny
on Belstead Hill. Keith says he's Captain Scott
because it's his sledge. I'm on the front.
He's on the back, his arms and legs around me.

Reading Week

Being and Nothingness was a brick. No wonder
I slept deeply in my old room, and never heard

Buzz and Dad going off to work on the roads.
In the evenings though, I knew they were here:

loud in the kitchen, I could smell their sweat
and the concrete that stuck to their clothes.

The living room shrank when they came in.
Dad stretched out, his feet on the coffee table,

Buzz snorted at the title of my book, turned
on the telly and sprawled across the sofa.

Awake early on the Friday, I watched
their van's tail lights disappear,

and at the station, Mum and I waved goodbye
until my train entered the tunnel.

JUNE CREBBIN

Encounter

Sorry, it wasn't me who climbed the steps of the Duomo
to see the whole of Firenze spread out below,
I didn't attempt the tower of Pisa either
Or pose for the obligatory photo.

I thought about the summit of Mt.Teidi,
but 'Persons with Breathing Difficulties should not ... etc.'
Certainly you wouldn't find me in a night club
in Los Americanos – far too exciting.

White water rafting? In Wales? Definitely not me.
I'm more your ocean cruise type of person.
Watendlath? I've been but never walked over the hill
into Borrowdale.

I was in the Shetland Isles last summer –
at Sumburgh Head. You were? Well, that's it then.
I braved the cliff edge to see those puffins.
Thanks. I'll have a white wine and soda.

alone in the house

while I am folding his pyjamas
making the bed
tidying the room
ready for his return

he is

while I am dusting
leaning against his piano
seeing the ring on my finger
catching the light

he is

while I am resting
in the middle of the day
considering the child
soon to be born

while I am answering the door
to the policeman
telling him I am alone
in the house

ELIZABETH CHADWICK PYWELL

For Zoe

If there was one good reason
why I'd paint my nails again,
it wouldn't be because of renewed interest,
or adding a bit of bling before a holiday,
or even to experience the audacity
of choosing Chilli Pepper Red or Pistachio Green,
but because a small child,
taking my hands in hers,
running her fingers over each satin surface,
said: 'I love your nails.'

English Teacher Blues

My first year teaching, I read Noughts & Crosses
with my third form & at the end I cry –
they're a little taken aback. I say, *he's just a child*,
& they look at me with their child eyes & child hearts,
& I look back with mine. The bell rings.
The year after that it's Mister Pip, fed to the pigs.

I cry for Private Peaceful & his brother, for everyone
in the Heart of Darkness, which is our whole world,
for Mercutio, Joe Keller, Medea's babies, Ophelia,
countless others. My reputation: the one who cries a lot.
I cry for Peter too, for Beth, for André, Jess.
In the staffroom, on the phone, in the Abbey church.

How to explain that a death in the family is never less
than a death in the family. I love you all. Be safe.

PAULINE PLUMMER

Corkscrew

I was forty.
Gordon bought me one that had won a design award,
shaped as an expanding fish of gleaming steel.
When you twisted and turned the hook into the cork
the fish concertinaed and spread like a fat guppy.

When you held the bottle between knees and pulled
it became a long thin barracuda, biting the cork
out of the neck.

It has opened many bottles. Gordon thought I drank too much.
It sleeps flat in the utensils drawer crushed by
Kitchen Devils, graters, slotted spoons, fish slicers.
There are few bottles with corks now.
They remind me of the cork plantations in Andalusia
near the farmhouse where I worked for a rich American
who hobnobbed with the Francoist aristocracy.
They owned the plantations.

The workers who tended and harvested the cork wore
patched blue clothing,
like Miguel who trapped a pigeon and stewed it.
He uncorked cheap red wine with his teeth.
I ate it with him in his hut. One reason why I got sacked.
Gordon is dead.

JACCI BULMAN

Altocumulus clouds

We stood and looked up at the '*altocumulus lenticularis*',
stood together at the gates to the caravan park, and yeah,
some of us took photos, others pointed, stared,
and we said how amazing it was,
like a visit from a UFO.
But we didn't quake with fascination
at the fantasticness of it all because,
right then, our lives – presumed to be
immortal and due to continue this free –
were also fantastic.
So, we laughed, looked up, lit cigarettes,
then went back to our caravans,
or the beach, or wherever we felt like going,
under the starships.

JOHN GOODBY

Mr Fisher Sits In
i.m. Roy Fisher (1930-2017)

Now class, this is Mr Fisher. He is
a special teacher, one who teaches other
teachers. Yes, teachers have to learn things too.
He is here today to observe your lesson
with Miss Parker. Be on your best behaviour
and give Miss Parker your full attention –
at which the owner of this voice
departs.
               Which is a fiction. Mr Fisher,
however, now sits at the back of the classroom.
His jacket will be corduroy, perhaps; vaguely
green-grey. Trousers, vaguely grey-green.
He will be clean-shaven, as that
was his life-long preference; mildly-spoken,
with what my mother calls *an educated
local accent*. Probably he has a briefcase.
In it, a book and his lunch. Sandwiches, egg-
and-cress. William Carlos Williams. Perhaps
he travelled here by bus, the 67,
crawling from the city, via congested Hockley
and Handsworth, out to where the city thins
in suburbs, Perry Barr, Great Barr, Kingstanding,
on its way to Pheasey.
                     Over his crossed leg,
let's say, a notebook reclines, and in his hand,
in his left hand, he holds a short red pencil.
                                 This
is realism, and he considers it.
                         Meanwhile
Miss Parker – in cat's-eye glasses, white blouse,
navy knee-length skirt, with dark, curly hair –
gazes towards him nervously. At his nod
she begins.
               Imagining that lesson
is beyond us, although I do know Porky Bagshaw
will put his used chewing-gum in the pockets
of Miss Parker's beautiful blue blazer one break,
and that I came on her in tears, red-faced, once,
muttering 'Bloody kids!' She had a sharpness of eye,
of voice, I liked, even though I was biddable and
her vulnerability came as a shock.
                           Details
could easily be laboured. Dip-in inkwells,
wooden, steel-nibbed pens; our allotted desks
with lids to slam shut, *bang!*, times tables gun-
tacked to the walls; the poster about vitamins
and all the colourful foods they inhabited
over the washbasins by the outside toilets;
those *Look & Learn*s in a glass cabinet; the gerbil
in its tank; the absence of black or brown faces;
the sweaters and shorts, and milk and cocoa
in the winter; scent of cedar pencil shavings;
chalkdust; sugar paper; rank, sprouting beans,
and Victory Vs – but I won't, even though
they are listed here. Our hands go up too easily
after shuffling in from the queue by the door
to endorse such easy nostalgia, the pathos
of an embroidered loss as lyric.
                         Mr Fisher,
who we have neglected, forgotten even, stands
as the bell goes, picks up his briefcase,
speaks briefly to Miss Parker and vacates
the premises.
               He got what he came for.

ORLAGH O'FARRELL

Relation

All I know about him is
that he grew up in Skerries
amongst the gulls and waves
with a hot-tongued mother
and a sea captain father

that he and his brothers all went to sea
that he was handsome
the girls had an eye for him
though not he for them

that he drowned in the quicksands off Newry
where the boat had put in
with a cargo of limestone
from the quarries at Milverton

that the boat bearing his body
sailed back down the coast
arrived in Skerries on the Thursday before Easter

that the whole town came to the beach
to stand in silence
as the boat came in.

Uncle Dessie

He always used to wear a flat cap
my uncle on that side

his face under it always lit
by a huge smile.

"Go way!" he'd say a lot,
in reaction to something interesting
you told him

shaking his head as if to marvel at
your knowledge.

The constant world was
interesting to him,
full of things to wonder at

and if they were really something

"Go way out of that!" he'd say
his eyes wide, a delighted smile
on his cap-crowned happy face.

MAITREYABANDHU

Beaudesert and Swancroft

A moan from her bedroom but when I go in
she's asleep again, protected by… who knows?
Larry pops over, stands, shuffles, enquires –
"Keep the heat in" he says, closing the kitchen door
on the odds and sods her garden doesn't need.
Gameshow. Advert. The bungalow settling
to its vigil while I do the washing up.
"What did your last slave die of?" my mother asks
inside my head as the barometer drops.
I switch the lights off. The moon shines weakly
on the tarmac as I go to bed with no dog
sleeping in the passageway to guard us,
just a few stars over Beaudesert and Swancroft.

TIM DOOLEY

Waking,

I struggled to remember
the word the assessor had used
that seemed to capture and excite
the minds of our colleagues.

It could have been
successionism or *superintendence,*
cross-briefing or *concapitulation.*

I knew I was out of the loop.

Anxious to undermine what was
happening, I could have sown
scepticism by the coffee urn
with slants of the head and silence,
but puzzled instead with etymology.

If I could undo the word,
would we be safe? (Or saved?)
Did I call that meeting?

All I know is I spoke from my chair
denouncing the word
then looked up at my audience.

The empty plastic seats.
And standing to the left my old supervisor,
smiling, shaking her head in frustration.

And outside, men dismantled fences
making the palings weapons,
missiles against order and law.
Arms raised, pointing, shouting,
setting fires as the night came on.

SUE RILEY

Waking to Oranges

On that first morning she woke
a stranger in a strange place.
The sun was hot. She heard
voices she could not understand.
Someone out there called Ola! Ola! Naranjas!
Almost a song.
She leaned from her window,
saw a man along the road leading a donkey
carrying baskets of oranges, lemons and melons.
He waved his hat, a straw hat.
Hey! she called out. Oranges, please. Over here.
He stopped beneath the window,
lifted up his hat full of fruit. She opened her arms
to receive the offering. How much?
He waved his hat.
Tomorrow, he said, tomorrow.
And led his donkey away
up the street, calling as he went,
Ola! Naranjas!

Frog Morning

It's early, bright with morning sun
A small boy is prowling the garden
with a butterfly net.
The air is loud with gulls on rooftops.
The boy drops his net, kneels,
reaches under the hedge.
He rises, walks steadily to the house
hands cupped around his find.
His father puts a clear plastic box on the patio
pours in a cup of water. The boy
opens his hands and a frog hops
into the water. The boy leans
over the box, eyes on the frog.
The frog is still, its eyes on the boy.

JULIE LUMSDEN

Welcome to Nottingham

Yes, yes, fabulous flying visit
to Five Leaves Bookshop, avoiding
the old haunts, deaf
to arguments and laughter
in that 70's kitchen, blind to that garden
where flat-out cats enjoyed summer days
and a sapling became a tree.
Leaf shadow on a particular wall, twigs
criss-crossing into runes
which advise us to move north.
Who knows the moment when things begin to change?
That house grew tired of our shabbiness.
A city drew a line under us and moved on.

LORRAINE Mc ARDLE

Princess Magic Touch™ Presumed Dead

I thought you were the one who got away,
buried in a funeral game we saw as fun.

But I forgot to mark your tomb
and when playing in the sand was done,

you were gone. I spent all summer digging,
burying you deeper I suppose, and still

you were not found, the ground
opened up and swallowed you whole.

Did you tell the worms and earwigs,
hear harebell roots ringing of your demise?

Did slugs come out at night and wiggle
their slimy slithery antennae?

Or did you cry yourself to sleep
with sandy soil to dry your eyes?

I buried you deep my childhood doll,
not realising that you were really gone.

Looking for your likeness years later
on eBay and Amazon, not quite accepting

that you were done. And then, long
after those lost summers and endless days,

the earth shifted and you poked your head out
through a dandelion spray. With the tip of a spade

you came back only slightly grazed,
the memory I had buried in a shallow grave.

IAN POPLE

Even the dock

At the end of autumn, a thin layer of snow on the streets,
when even the dock had a skimming of ice, the mallards

gathered on the spillway, fighting for bread, a small child
throwing it, his blue coat unbuttoned and dancing in time

with each throw, and one who would lean back on a stick
and look up at the guttering, or sit in spring in another's

garden where echinacea gazes fatly into the sun, when the hebe
draws the wasps, theirs the certainty of grubbing among the foliage,

and us, one parent and one child, the before, the after, and the
as well, where the studded white of hedgerow flowers is the edge.

MAGGIE REED

these bright moments
i.m. John Foggin

chaplets of snowdrops glow
under hawthorn

sharp slant sun
over bright trickling beck

aconites under alder
by the stile to the woods

five lawns wait for next
summer's lawnmowers

a curlew from the marshes
mourns the pale moon

an honesty seed-pod
caught in January sky

NIA BROOMHALL

On Sitting

At forty-five I stop sitting down. I want
to be up. My hands start to prickle if
they are not moving, or holding. I want
to be up. And I remember my mother

at forty-five, how it made me twitch
that she would not stay still, singing,
knitting, putting out prickled arms
and filling jars and grinning, bristling,

shifting furniture, trimming salt dough
and fringes, stripping walls, filling the car
boot, nipping-in her uniform, driving out
of the drizzle in search of sun, twisting

the cone for mr-whippied drips, licking
stamps, pinning the green phone under
her chin and stringing pictures and gifts
in scissor-curled ribbon and I remember

her mother, then, her fidgeting and tea.
I can see it now, why. We can't waste
it. We want to slip the knots and flick
the lights and click in glittered shoes

and spit the truth. We'll hold. I want to
put out arms like milk-thistles and mugs.
I want to stitch bright Xs that spell, in
my mum's handwriting, how to stay up.

Horses

Her days were gates to be
opened, or gates to be cleared,
on a big horse that wants to

clear them, that pelts forward
and lands with a blood-
pumping thump in some field

full of things it wants to see.
That's how her days were,
every last one of them, even

the last one of them. And
there are horses, and fields full of
hoof-prints, full of gleaming rain.

JEAN STEVENS

Hooves
24 April 2024

Here come the revelation horses,
among them, the fastest two,
one black, one white, with blood streaking
from mane to tail and dripping
from panicked feet, galloping for miles,
colliding with a taxi, and smashing
the windscreen of a double decker bus,
spooked by noises that never came from nature
and racing over London's fields seeking
the grass buried beneath the tarmac,
their hooves drilling down
to hidden rivers and ancient forest.
Ahead of them lie the wonders of St. Paul's
and, under them, the wild things that we've lost.

Bucket List

Number one is getting a tattoo.
I imagine a dark chemical smell,
the pain of a needle scoring my flesh,
the tattooist pulling my ageing skin taut
wiping off blood and surplus ink.

He's painting a peacock butterfly,
that being of velvet and flame,
with eye-spots blue as the sky,
whose wings when closed become
the dead leaves of autumn.

I've chosen two creatures in one,
the peacock, earthbound since
its flight feathers were clipped,
and the butterfly which *can* fly.
Both in the crook of my welcoming arm.

FOKKINA McDONNELL

Landscape with a footbridge

A rickety wooden structure, this footbridge.
No wonder the horses are doubtful; the one
supporting a nobleman (large black hat)
prances, if that is the right word.
His companion stands facing our way.
He isn't paid to think. His fiery red robe
is a highlight in the painting: the noble trees,
spreading roots of romanticised countryside.
Half-hidden, a man may be fishing.

All three are 400 years away from you.
Now, they'd be wearing pullovers
and waders. The nobleman would
have parked the SUV, relied on GPS.
But they too would have been stopped
by the sight of the narrow footbridge,
the loose planks, the drop at least
four metres, the water too shallow.

Note: Jacob van Ruisdael, *landscape with a footbridge*, 1652.

Take my advice,

Dotty, don't join the U3A.
There's nowhere to park in Didsbury.
They don't have a meeter-and-greeter.
You'll stand stock still, staring into
the middle distance with a frozen smile.

It's a cliché, Dotty, but they're
elderly, white middle-class and
you'll be expected to pretend and run
Italian language classes while being judged
on the standard of your carrot cake.

There's no alcohol at this Tuesday
meeting, only stale tea, bitter coffee.
Tables to attract you to sub-groups
of Ping-Pong, Arts & Crafts, German for
beginners. Dotty, *nein, nein, nein.*

There are no men. That's a lie, Dotty.
They're being taken, reeled in like fat fish
by committee members who grow
carnations. Dotty, *bleib zu Hause.*
Pour a Malbec and watch Monty Don.

BARBARA MARSH

Wild horses
i.m. Debi O'Hehir

She loved horses. Everyone knew that,
her flat filled with drawings, on paper, on wood, paintings,
sculptures of horses, tall, spindly-legged, so thin
an observer could worry they would break,
wild horses, young and fluid, cantering across fields,
sitting before sleep, some winged, not *in* flight
but perhaps considering,
not-quite-taut enough to take off yet.
She rode her bike everywhere, cigarette
between her fingers. Always moving,
ambidextrous, both hands drew the contours
and ambitions of each wild, thin, impossibly tall horse,
each ready to race out of the field, or fly to who knew where.
Each fragile, and almost unbreakable.

18th arrondissement

You walk down the short hall to the front room, your
body yoga-light, your mind quiet, to join the others
at the kitchen bar. Croissants on the counter, Myriam
asks if you want coffee and serves it in a small cup,
with one sugar. It's an unaccustomed treat, usually you
take green tea but it's Paris, you're in Montmartre,
you're in love with the people walking past the front
window of this apartment, the soft French vowels in
the chatter on the street. Eric slices a pineapple they
bought from the shop next door and puts the round
yellow circles on a plate. The taste is like your early
childhood next to the Pacific, plumeria in the air and
the sweet scent of *ananas* in your hands, as you eat
round the scaly peel. Eric changes the album to Nancy
Sinatra and Lee Hazelwood, and he and Steve talk
about turntables. Everything is new, this place, these
people, your miraculous friendship that has blossomed
like the crown of this pineapple. You all get your coats
on to ward off the December chill, and head out,
Steve and Eric now discussing speakers, and you hook
your arm through Myriam's, simple as that.

TERRY QUINN

Almost approaching the station

After fields and cows, a train ticks past ours
on parallel tracks. A man is wearing a party hat.
A child breathes on the window and writes
something backwards to me, like a name
on the other side of a mirror.

On Bare Lane Station

I don't know where
the two of them were going
but I'd got off early
the stop before Morecambe
a walk along the Prom
tea at the Midland Hotel

but then came a question
from the youngster
hand in hand with her dad

Tell Me The Facts About Anything

well good luck with that mate
was my immediate thought
and I tied my shoelaces
to give me time
for them to get ahead
as I knew I'd say something
if he didn't say anything

and then I'd have to apologize
for butting in
try to make some excuse
that didn't involve saying
that I wish I could be
showing my own child
how to pour tea
at the Midland Hotel.

PAUL MILLS

Pastoral

Saturday and Tom and Chris are fishing
wet entangled branches down to the edge
early spring at the end of the pike season.

The dawn chorus they tell me
was an explosion, and when I join them
threads of it are still here.

I stand looking at shoots of new moss
ground spread with wild garlic leaves
deep in the woods.

Mud from a recent flood
like glue to walk through.

Across slow-moving windless water
the great garden of the country house,

a daffodil-shock on the far bank,
so many known tree-species
under the eye of Lady Evelyn Compton
who could be looking at us
and perhaps is.

I'm glad I'm here.
Herons, an otter, cormorants, kingfishers
seem to belong to this side of the river.

Twigs near us are budding with drops of rain.

A pike, gripped on the bank, deep-hooked,
and for minutes you are two workmen,
two surgeons, the patient
so patient, blood in its gills.

Desperate to restore it, but you can't. The barbs hold.

You let it go. Perhaps the river will
in its own time shake them loose.

A gift, the movement of spring renewing
but for how long?

The future, once weightless distance
tilts forward. Everywhere is an edge.

A year of rain
hangs in a single cloud.

DAVID UNDERDOWN

My street

is steep. The top is halfway up the hill
where the builders lost their bottle.

The street stretches like a helping hand
to lead you up through its contours.

The postie with asthma hates it
but it helps to keep him going.

Like any street it is a collection of houses
that leads from somewhere to somewhere else.

Over the valley, trees patrol the skyline.
Later they cast shadow-fingers down its sides.

Some of the houses are loved, others are having a hard time
but at night all are guarded by the genies of the lamps.

In an old photo a dark-haired girl
is leaving my front door. It is already sixty years ago.

My street has two parts like the window-cleaner's ladder:
the lower half has a pavement, then there are steps.

If this was a fairy story, a dragon
would hide at the top of the steps.

By day the street is a sandy shade of Pennine stone
until, one night, it was silvered by a winter moon.

My street was once a bare hill.
Soon it may be a forest. Or a desert.

The forecasts are grim. The Council has delivered salt.
The bin-men have been told to fear the worst.

The Homecoming
After 'Hunters in the Snow' by Pieter Breughel the Elder

You'll know the one I mean: a painting of many pictures
held whole by snow below a green grey sky.

Remember how the ground drops steeply
down to the valley and its small town.
On these short days it's snow provides the light.
Far off, jagged crags, dark woodlands, copses
but in the middle ground a meandering river
has spilled its bounds to flood the meadows.
Ice has become a thoroughfare: children skate,
sledge, chase dogs. Someone struggles with an umbrella.
Men with chapped hands are picking their way home.

Like an altar-piece, bare trunks of trees
make windows for us to view the scenes beyond.
If you could telescope across the snow-clad roofs
past shutters shadowed by jutting gables
aproned women, broad hipped, would be kneading bread,
a grandfather dozing by the embers of a stove.

But this is only part of it for three figures
have reached the edge of the canvas
and now burst into sight, dark on light.
They mean business with their staves and pikes.
One has a flintlock strapped across his shoulder.
Their motley pack of deadbeat hounds
drag their tails across the snow like cursive script.
No one has seen them yet, but these men
who trudge with aching calves and chilblained hands,
are heroes returning to their Ithaca.

Above, a harbinger, a slim-winged falcon
swoops ahead with tidings of their arrival.
Already their thoughts are in the kitchen's warmth.
They smell the meaty stew that's waiting on the stove.

MEG COX

Not Quite

She lived in Willesden Green
within walking distance of Hampstead Heath
nearly but not quite
She stayed in Chatou in West Paris to learn French
nearly but not quite
She went for drinks in the top flat of a tower block
and met a man who tried to seduce her
nearly but not quite (unfortunately!)
She moved to a village in Herefordshire
which was a few miles from Wales
nearly but not quite
She knew what the road to Hell was paved with

Despite

if I didn't like the tattoos that men have
if I didn't like men who had hairy backs
if I didn't like men with hairy chests
if I didn't like kissing men with full beards
if I didn't like men who were shorter than me
if I didn't like men who were bald like my father
if I didn't like men who smoked
if I didn't like men who wore bow ties
if I didn't like men who wore vests
if I didn't let any of that stop me
well, you only live once

MIKE DI PLACIDO

Another poem about David Hockney

He was on the evening news at 6.
Large as life, at eighty-odd, smiling
and flashing his crocs, drawling on
about his new installation at Tate Modern
in a yellow checked suit, as though he was
a living billboard for his own art.
I was reminded of the day on Brid Beach –
which is next door to us, more or less – him,
ambling along in his white linen suit
and Panama hat (he used his mum's house
in the town as a studio for years). I went up
and asked if he'd doodle me a seagull
and put his moniker at the bottom, 'cos
I fancied a wild month in Marbella.
He just laughed out loud, shook his head
and waddled off. He did laugh, though –
I'll give him that. He did laugh.

Vertiginous at Opening Time
The Spa Bridge, Scarborough.

Comical and odd, no doubt, to the passers-by:

a duffel-coated figure, with hood up and head down,
going hell for leather down the middle of the bridge
in the late morning sun.

But how could they know of my desperate and ingenious plan
of slaying two dragons in one – vertigo and delirium tremens –
in getting to my favourite pub for the first of the day.

JOHN LANCASTER

An Attendance Officer Calls
i.m. Geoff Hattersley

To write in English dialect is an innately political act, an assertion against the ever-increasing spread of received pronunciation and the privilege underpinning it (Matthew Paul on Geoff Hattersley)

We heard his Austin thunging as it jounced down our divilin track

with mother mithered sick, as Eric Bath, always off with his chest, had been put forward by him for a boys' home on the Blackpool coast

to build him up. She sided the jerry pot, plumped fresh, aired pillows as swobsy Mr Robinson's trilby bobbed past iced-up windows.

Let in, I could hear him stamping the flothery snow off his shoes, ask, *What's it this time? Idleitis?* And she gave him the bad news

I'm made away with pneumonia. Putting his hat on a chair, he hutched over me, ex-police suspicious, wary, silver hair

middle-parted like all men back then, arrow-straight with
        the ronk smell
of shiny Brylcreem overpowering his hope that I'd be well

to sit the eleven-plus and though ever likely on the mend all but a fortnight bedfast naturally meant I'd dropped behind

the others. But no need to feel werrit or any shame at that he would get me workbooks from school, bring them over
        just now. He sat

his fat arse to unlock an important-looking briefcase then wrote in a file, *To let them know you're not trying it on.* As a joke.

But it put us in a mind of guilt and blame, mother all mimsy and seeming sneaped, accused of not looking after me properly;

my crime, wagging it as badly. Done, snapping the bag's brass clasp shut, he messed off, car coughing choke-out fumes revved to tackle frozen ruts.

Trial over, on the wireless Ken Dodd's jokes from Workers' Playtime bucked me up a treat, felt like clogging it away, escape, go climb,

sledge down Wickenstones. Before he came checking up again and off the penicillin, I'd lommered through drifts to the rocks at the top,

my way to show him I wasn't a nesh, mardy, lozzucking hullock.

Uncredited

Nosey neighbour; Latin noblewoman;
cocktail drinker; circus audience member;
Presbyterian; village woman (twice);
party guest; wedding guest; Mary's aunt;
French journalist; wet woman; opera fan;
Sokovian driver; housewife. Voiceless

about what you were given, but handy too
as you had to live within the M25, be on call
for makeup by five then costumed, herd-ready
on ten quid an hour from budgets of millions.
No choice after he left: friends did school runs
but she would always be there to pick me up
with catering van treats smuggled out inside
a smuggled coat. The rewards. The glamour.

The director of a flop tried it on – she had
a beautiful mouth, might be a speaking part.
When she shoved him off he said her voice
sounded like a cat pissing in a biscuit tin,
she'd never make it, would see to it. And did
as work dried up, apart from role-playing stuff
for trainee doctors – *students had to say, we
have to insert a catheter in Mr Smith's penis,
we need your authority. And I had to say, fine
as long as you can find it, watch as the tutor
assessed their reaction. No laughter allowed.*
The dramatic life. The making ends meet.

She looked back at wasting too much time
worrying about what her folks thought of her
doing such work, wasting that RADA degree,
not being able to hold down a full-time job.
It all only made sense each Christmas when
they showed that blockbuster again, on the sofa
with the kids waiting to spot her, asking,
Granny, where's Sokovia? And laughters.
The best part: worth it all, I told her.

STEPHEN PAYNE

Puddings

Puddings are the subject of today's 'Food Programme', which is playing on the car radio. I hear the presenter ask, "What do puddings tell us about what it means to be human?" after which I find it hard to listen. I slow down for a roundabout. All I'm getting from the show is an occasional word or phrase — tapioca, ceramic bowl, Buxton pudding. The lap belt pinches my belly flesh but I'm back on that philosophical question. Is it something to do with sensory pleasures that incur a cost? Ukrainian cheesecake. Food historian. Now I'm wondering about him, the only male voice I've noticed so far. Whether he collaborates with his colleague, the military historian. Perhaps they meet over lunch to discuss the diets of the great and brutal armies. Hannibal's sweet tooth. Mark Antony's recipe for tyropatina.

PAM THOMPSON

To Brighton Pier

        and I want to speak of moorings
   of being grounded.
What insights about the sea churning
   under you reach me without speech? Collapsed
and hidden, lights, the Wheel of Fortune, ornate
Victorian benches. Is it night?

Are there futile chains
   across your entrance? Or have you broken
with your history, with what the crowd expects,
  and dimmed yourself, folding back into the city
   like any sea-front hotel I walk out of
and everything wordless (worthless?)
assumes a new shape.

ROBERT ETTY

Wednesday

Finding nothing other to do
than walk in the shade of horse chestnut trees

away from town with his eyes to the ground
and cars to his left and cows to his right,

he picks out on the mossed-over pavement
and picks up and holds on two fingertips

a willow warbler (or is it a chiffchaff),
dry, perfect and staring upward

at splaying leaves
lit by pink and white candles,

its birdflesh and bones, its death and feathers
unweighable on the scale of a hand.

ROBERT HAMBERGER

Rich Man Poor Man

Someone says I look like the man selling
cherries outside the station, although he's
bigger than me. Could I climb inside his life,
steal his cherries? Might they slip into my
mouth, so my teeth split open their shiny
skin and purple juice runs? Beggar man
thief. I want his job, shouting about a pound
of cherries, twisting the ends of brown
paper bags, spitting stones. I want
the home he walks back to every
evening, once his cherries are gone.
Who meets him at the door? Does anyone?
Will the taste of cherries occupy his dreams?

VASILIKI ALBEDO

Schnapps

It is Christmas, or her birthday,
or there's no reason at all for this party.
Mum claps as a gangly boy drinks
schnapps out of my slingback,
asks him if I look like her. We are both
blonde in this narrow moment of time
and side-by-side in our singleness,
she squishes her cheek on my cheek,
two peaches in saltwater, her call
cheers to whatever. Someone snapped
this photo I'm holding— here she is,
ten years on, pinching my cheek till it splits.

Pamplona

I'm in the wild pulse of the crowd
thrashing from within. Sunflowers
spill from balconies, streets line up
under crowded windows like a vice.

In the arena, the matador slices off
the bull's ear and gives it
to a woman on the stands.
It is his gift to her, this music
of a silenced life. I think of Vincent
offering his ear to Rachel as a bloom.
He, whose painting was a kind
of faith, who wanted 'something infinite,
something deep, something real'
and could not find it here.

CHRISTY KU

Homecoming
After Joung Young-Ju: The Living City

Village girl city grown
levitates from the gallery floor,
the shrinking shadow is a blame shaped child

called home through ink to a place
her parents have left and longed for.
When does a centre of gravity shift across land masses?

Is this seasickness or
homesickness or
a false nostalgia?

Home is a village you have not been to,
a house overgrown with neglect,
a pile of rubble and decade old arguments.

Blue roofs, yellow-white lights.
The blamed child wants to know
if the lights turn on any more.

LIZ BYRNE

Headless

I'll leave my head in Kinsale,
perch it on a weed-covered rock
on that small island in Sandycove.
I'll swim there, see for the last time
the glassy, green water, clear
as ice, seals and cormorants;
the island almost filling
the open mouth of the bay.

I'll unscrew my head,
pop it off, balance it
just above the high tide mark,
a thin square of dark chocolate
with a hint of sea-salt in my mouth
to be going on with.
I'll swim back to the mainland
where there is no pain.

CHARLOTTE WETTON

Bureau de Change

I have lost or forgotten my straw boater
and this uniformed official with the lugubrious moustaches
will not swap my French francs
for the life of a novelist (male novelist) with a wife
who makes a simple lunch of bread, cheeses, cold meats, tomatoes,
almonds, figs and watered wine.

*Look, will you not take Italian lire
for an encounter on an overnight sleeper
and a packet of Gauloises?*

I'm afraid not, Madam.

*Not for travellers' cheques? Not for a university degree and this
Grade 4 piano?*

No, Madam.

The sun is hot in the little square with the white shutters.
I retreat to the *brasserie*, knock back *un petit café* and marshal
my resources.

I cross back to the Bureau with a winning smile.
*Could you take this pile of laundry and this parking-ticket
for a blue bicycle with a kitten in a basket?*

We have no bicycles, Madam, only Euros.
His basset hound eyes are filled with regret.

It's not an unreasonable transaction, I say, my voice rising,
*this Coding for Beginners certificate
for a fling with a call girl and the moon rising over the cypresses.
I demand to speak to your superior.*

I have no superior, Madam.

At least the cypresses?
I'm pleading now.

*I'm sorry, Madam, what you have already cashed
exceeds the value of your account –*

But the simple lunch with the cold meats and the –

He holds up a hand.
*Madam, you are trying to affect the impossible. We do not permit
infinite exchanges.
Furthermore, we are now closed for siesta.*
And he pulls down the blind.

The sun glares down on the striped awnings of the market square,
my tongue smells of coffee.
A *V* of geese flies North.

ROD WHITWORTH

Alternative medicine

While waiting, you watch *Homes Under the Hammer*
next to the sign that tells you
    The current wait time is
    4 hours and 30 minutes
and *Escape to the Country,* an episode of each
before *they,* halfway through a presenter's smile,
switch the screen to public service announcements
about masks, how well the hospital trust does against
its performance targets and other places to get medical help.

The bloke next to you, cradling
his broken left arm
across his chest, confides
Yeah. I should've gone
to the pharmacy with this
or maybe the nail bar.

Calan the light-carrier

He was scrawny, maybe wiry, carried
two buckets, one each end of the pole
across his shoulders. *Light!* he shouted
I have light. Light to buy, beg or borrow!

People queued: children, women and men
queued, holding out their cupped hands.
Calan beamed, took his scoop, dipped
and poured a measure for one and all.

And the pouring, in and of itself,
lit up their faces, lightened their feet.
Each reached out, emptied their hands
over their neighbour. And everyone danced.

MARY NOONAN

Weather

Perched, curl-toed, on my corner of the sofa
I open my phone's Weather app,
skim the places we visited:

Milan, Rome, Clonmany, Ottawa.
It's a cold night everywhere, but
the night sky in Clonmany catches my eye –

digital snowflakes on a loop.
I feel the soft flakes on my face, see them
landing on ribs of carved limestone

in a dark graveyard.
I look to my right, see you as you were
when we sat up late, watching our favourites –

Homeland or *Breaking Bad*, maybe. But you're lying
under a stone at the far end of the country
and software is showing me what's going on with you.

I exit the portal, climb the stairs.
You always hated sleep, those dead hours.
Little amuse-bouches of snow-dusted oblivion.

At the Bassins de Lumières

The Nazi U-boat bunker on the edge of Bordeaux
is now a digital gallery, and they're showing Paul Klee.

Klee was your favourite. You're here in his anarchic
pinks and blues as they wash, in coded play

over the water bays, and goldfish do syncopated
jazz moves with moustachioed men in bowler hats.

Your voice is in my ear, saying 'If I win the lottery
I'll buy a submarine – it's a great way to travel.'

U-boats haunted your dreams – those prowling
the war-time coast of Donegal, or the ghost-boats

of the Hollywood films you watched as a boy
in the company of three bachelor uncles at Ballyliffin.

In this watery lurking-place for subs,
curated music can't muffle the pings of sonar

bouncing off the massive concrete pens.
Underwater phantoms are moving in flotillas

round the bunker. Klee mans a conning-tower,
scans the basin of light for traces of you.

SIÚN CARDEN

Scale Model

You know it's one of his before you see the name.
It makes the other boats look flat, their painted planks
thoughtless repetition.

In his galley, a tiny tap. A sharp knife.
Doors you could walk through, ropes you could pull,
the right weight in your arms

if you were the fleshy twin
of his homunculus, this fisherman
whittled with unreasonable care,

alive as the votive ships that float by northern pulpits,
suspended in hope or thanks on waves of prayer.

MICHAEL HENRY

Making Nice

The Personnel Manager had
a calibrated ruler on his desk.
    He checked my calculations, payslips
    and re-counted the canteen takings.

A good man formed by God, badminton
and the Territorial Army,
    he had an immaculate head
    of right-parted light-grey hair.

He invited his trainee managers
for High Tea in his Edwardian house
    where he lived in sibling celibacy
    with his slightly younger sister.

At one point he asked her permission
to take off his air-force blue jacket.
    Their wrinkles were kindly wrinkles
    from a constant drill of smiling

and he had an immaculate
parade of Pepsodent-white teeth.
    Two hours making nice and then
    we calculated it was time to go.

I backed my car at an awkward angle,
denting his racing-green garage door.
    He was very nice about it. As always.
    Nice to the nearest fraction of an inch.

LYDIA HARRIS

translating the prone woman
(female burial, Links of Pierowall Norse burial site, Westray)

i

you tell me nothing is translatable but I do it any way

a code in runes reads
my long time elder
turned to the moon
to the absence of moon

ii

I grant one extra hour to the prone woman

she follows the road
ignoring all side turnings
crosses the burn on the seven boulders

walks the sunken way to the col
weaves between birch rowan
and hazel only the aspen is missing

iii says the moon

please come
with your raindrop eye
your sagging cloud gown

swing across the firth
you   grubby smutched
but not with shame

she's a flute

barely a ghost
of sound

a bubble
rises

tucked behind
pressed lips

tunes her bones
brighter sharper

tests their tones
as they quiver air

her ears favour
deeper weightier

sounds made
light trimmed

ice in her pith
the come and go

the tide pull
she drifts

out of reach
notes of a song

she can't remember
long gone

you were the words for *silence* and for *nothing*

a length of grey cloth grazed your face

beacons lit the dunes where they laid you

your body sailed you from the boat-house
crossed and re-crossed brae and wetland

when you broke open you escaped to the willow
took root   already ancient in boughs and offshoots
turning through leaves and catkins

buds plump with the life that clothed you
the you in that life

You led me

across the backland
over a layer of peat and wattle-work
hid from me the costrel   the six wooden combs

I dreamt I lifted the scallop shell
carried it over the watery places
past the moon-dripped gorse

you quickened me
as I climbed two gates
ducked three lengths of wire fence
crossed Tumbled-Ewe Field

I reached the Corn-house
its forestair to east
its crow-stepped gables

you made me to turn
my eyes to the trunk
twisted to a *u*   to a *u*

and an arc of red sand reached up to hold me
on wet wrack and storm-driven pebbles
and the sky with clouds pulled back

I had spoken with the broch
the wren and many mottled boulders
passed under and over
crossing from field to field

moving from yard to track
to shore   into the not-land of the ocean
and back again

what wrought the change in her

was it the sand
or the runes struck in the lead by her hand

was it the comb
the rivets on bone

was it the beaten floor of her grave

are those the things that make her less than she is

or is it that she alone lies face down

no boat or horse to help her across
no track to the well

no daughter there
her scriptures loosed to the air
her words songs no one can hear

LYDIA HARRIS CONTINUED

the prone woman speaks back

name me
by my footsteps

wait three breaths
three wave crashes

I rise from stony ground
walk narrow paths

watch with the hermit crab
in sand and gravel

withstand strong tideways
am grasped in roots of tangles

pass with me through that doorway
my words moored to rock crevices

do not overlook me

my mothers crossed the North Sea
in a swift boat with the smell of resin

JENNY KING

Woman with two greyhounds

The first greyhound, Hope, is white
with a neat head and soft whiskers.
She can run like the wind,
the breeze from a flowering pasture
carrying the scent of April.

The other, Darkness, is brown and taller.
Her ribs are like harp strings
plucking a dirge from the anonymous air.
She runs like the autumn wind
that snatches leaves from their anchor
and hurls them down.

The woman is waiting to cross the road.
She holds a lead in each hand,
looks one way then the other, crosses, pauses.
Which way will she turn today?
The dogs wait for her voice.

JON MILLER

Transient

Socrates was sat at the end of the bed
watching TV. God, he was ugly – boils,
flat-faced, reeking of fish as if he'd been
dragged head-first through centuries,
trainer on one foot, flip-flop on another.
He had a chihuahua on his lap.
I was dreading his signature Q&A
that would put me in an ethical headlock
at 3am but he reached into his giant
JD Sports bag and brought out a dodo,
Napoleon's tricorn, Shakespeare's quill,
a splinter of the True Cross, held them up
as if trying to remember where they came from.
He turned as if seeing me for the first time.
Showed no curiosity. Not a glimmer.
Stared, looked away. This is how it was now.
Like he'd seen enough, was just passing through
this burning century to some other horror,
rudderless, in limbo, knackered, and all out
of questions. He was channel-hopping,
watching catastrophes on repeat
(crashed economies, the yachts of the rich,
wildfires, helicopter crashes, avian flu)
when suddenly I thought this wasn't Socrates
but some homeless crackhead who'd
wandered in (had I locked up?) and who
even now was shuffling down the stairs
with his charity shop bargains on his way
to the embankment or the ventilators
back of Pizza Hut with my wallet,
while his bug-eyed mentalist chihuahua
purled out a tiny shit at the foot of the bed.
By the time I got downstairs he was gone,
just that stench of beached whale,
the odour of wisdom rotting in spacetime.

Old Flame

Once again they've blown my cover, the old lovers.
Out they come, rummaging these raging chambers,
pummelling the walls of my heart.

Late nights, I google your names, bounce them
round satellites but it's forty years since
and I'm hunched at a screen scouring

the wrong cheekbones, those flat heels
and summer shorts, that questionable hair dye,
blue eyes in tortoise-shell glasses.

We breathe on the glass of each other to check
we're still here, our futures a mist of pixels,
fireworks dissolving in a nameless sky. But maybe

when *Forever Young* comes on the radio
or *Madame George* as you pick up the kids from school
or football or, late summer, that last drink,

something wistful in the trees, husband cooking dinner,
I imagine you thinking of me as you remember
the men you had and how it all fell to earth here

in this garden, these sunset hills, after the teaching,
divorce, baptisms and weddings and now
the lump in the breast I once kissed.

BEN McGUIRE

What I Still Know About Procida

They made *Il Postino* among its circle of coves,
though Neruda had spent his time on Capri.

L'Isola di Arturo, which I started,
loved with such a worthy love and never finished,
is set there.

On Procida a waiter once described heroics to us,
state-defying feats
that meant he owed more than he could ever pay.
What those exploits were, I can't remember.

I can recall dappled lushness
in the hotel's vineyard with deckchairs,
prodigious lemons that someone gave us,
and – altogether elsewhere
in the span of a small island –
a ridge pointing
past prickly pears
at sea.

Procida is, in spite of this poem.

Procida will get you drunk.

Procida's a book I picked up once.

Procida is hazy with heroes.

The Way the Weeks Away Came Back

A woman juggling
at a back window our tram slid by.

A market, snuggled up to an *hypermarché*'s bulk.

The two of us, wired to the same music on the night coach.
Sleepy borders we were carried over.

The old man with the big rucksack crammed with empty bottles.
He stopped to rest his back. His gesture for more glass.

A plane droning into a tap's splash above our dorm; remembering
the first room, ours alone.

The lift up to Ivan's flat. A groan from somewhere. Growing –
then the button I had pressed in popped back out, a cannon shot.

Beside you on that high floor, still awake. Phrases in me, looping:
chasm of sleep, chasm of the street. And
sinking. Cyrillic metro-station runes. The first room.

The Sergiev Posad cathedral, a crucified Christ without poise,
and the saints dappling the walls like wine stains,
murals that ringed the bell tower. Up, on, out of sight.

Back home, I had to make myself at home,
memory still juggling the places
we'd catch-thrown.

JIM McELROY

Michael, Do You Ever Regret

never knowing your Latin amo or amat,
the daily dole-out of their slaps,
Bartlett's sweat beads on the sheen
of his pate, the smack of his cane
welting Greek on your palm, the rise
of their belts, the strappings in French,
thwacks on your hands for homework undone?
Or do you regret the half-smirk
of your cheek, the ice-blue of your eyes
staring them down, or lost out the window,
Humpy Malone's ruler
rapping your knuckles back to mathematics?

I felt the purple throb of your fingers,
your short fuse smouldering at the desk,
and under its lid the mince
of corned beef stinking your lunch box.
You sat up in science – Master Breen
clacking the forces of physics, static electricity,
the properties of matter, across the blackboard.

Do you regret how you ticked off the seconds
as the hand tocked to three
and the final bell rang, that you left,
served your time for a trade?
Electrics, wiring, that sort of thing,
Humpy said when I asked him.

And do you ever regret how you studied
the clock, got it wrong, how you packed
your lunch box, your too-short fuse
bedded down for the job,
the timer miss-set when you primed it,
your blue eyes blinded in the whoosh
of white light from homework undone:
how the head-splitting boom ripped prams
from their wheels, tore shopping bags, hands,
through the whine of the sirens, wha wha of alarm?

AMY DUGMORE

Zuihitsu on the joys of small breasts

1. I've always liked smallnesses. Doll's houses. Portrait miniatures. Tiny books, bottles of perfume. Miniscule worlds that hold their secrets close. Beg you, the pleasure-seeker, because you are always the pleasure-seeker, to look closer. Their secretness is pleasure.
2. The sort of barely-there whisper that says come find me.
3. Breasts. Yes. All of them. But mostly mine. Upturned magnolia cups. Trace veins against cream and pinkness.
4. Bee stings, rosebuds, all the clichés tucked into satin, softly pointed cups. The thrill of a first bra. Its secret clasp sharp against your skin.
5. How the slogan on my t-shirt is perfectly legible.
6. I scroll Google for images of Audrey Hepburn. Audrey in evening dress. Audrey in Breton top. Arms bare, arms covered. Diamonds. Audrey making an erogenous zone of clavicles. They sing like chords.
7. My breasts are inspirational! My niece tells her mother she wants breasts like mine when she's older. Unobtrusive. Unassuming. Overt shows of flesh make her queasy. She vetoes my choice of a one-shouldered evening dress – it might *make my boobs fall out*. Even my breasts can fall victim to gravity.
8. According to the Breast Size Satisfaction Survey (Elsevier, March 2020) 70.7% of women are unhappy with their breasts. Across 40 countries and tens of thousands of women my breasts are a rebellion.
9. Keira Knightley in green satin.
10. Keira complaining about the Pirates of the Caribbean promotional posters, how they photoshopped her slight chest into a cleavage.
11. Sometimes I think about the girls with bigger breasts who got paid to drape their bodies over cars on pedestals at weekends. Sold as glamour. Their bodies no sooner grown than claimed, commoditised. Don't get me wrong – they earned well, paid for new clothes, driving lessons and maybe I would've done it. My breasts spared me the question.
12. It takes me almost an hour to wipe the biro X from my skin. Marking what might lie beneath.
13. Against the petrol smell of gel, in a darkened room, ultrasound waves trace the curve, while two women look at blueish shapes on screens, shifting. The secrets within the secrets of my breasts are luminous.
14. I long for you to touch me again – I'd say just once but I'd be lying, your touch opening up a portal through me – soft, nipples, throat. Yes, the way you used to touch my breasts. The rise of them in my vest top enough to make you stutter
15. *The articulate is the enemy of the erotic.*
16. My breasts. Of late, like a sudden fruiting in surprise, so that I want to show you –
17. these. My theses are plenty but all conclude the same that if I could just show you these, you would be struck by the hint, you would unravel yourself so surely that I could stand back and watch over the tips of my newly risen nipples, feel the swell

Hero

In the heat of the tin can car,
sweat slipping down my thighs, your thighs
in shorts, we're sitting
because it's too hot to travel by any means except time
you tell me about this other July,
a younger you, stumbling into a corner shop stick-up
this guy grabbing Twixes, Mars Bars from the counter, yelling
for Bensons and Marlboros, for fivers and tenners, whatever's in the float, your
hair black then as you enter this scene
your lat muscles tensing as you pull back and swing
you want me to see bravery, biceps,
knowing I can't touch.
I'm scanning for the thermostat, some sign of season or celsius
because heat can make you do anything.

Because heat can make you do anything
I'm scanning for the thermostat, some sign of season or celsius,
knowing I can't touch.
You want me to see bravery, biceps,
your lat muscles tensing as you pull back and swing
your hair black then as you enter this scene
for Bensons or Marlboros, with fivers and tenners to add to the float,
this guy grabbing Twixes, Mars Bars from the counter, yelling
at a younger you stumbling into a corner shop stick-up
you tell me about this other July
because it's too hot to travel by any means except time.
In shorts, we're sitting,
sweat slipping down my thighs, your thighs
in the heat of the tin can car.

EILIS STANLEY

Cow day

Each spring, they bolt out of the barns,
like Beryl Cook ballet dancers
twirling in the new grasses;

heads gone with the madness of scents
and the shimmering seduction of daylight.
Red roan, chestnut, black and white,

jostling each other past broken gates
and rusting troughs, the ground of gravity
gone. They dance their winter bulk as if

all weight was a locked barn and freedom
the roar of pounding hooves in their wild,
spring spinning over the warming land.

ROSIE HADDEN

A night out in Tyrone circa April 1981

I'd crimped and dyed my hair silver
made up my face to match
blue lips and turquoise eyes
daubed my wellies with silver Hammerite
My sprayed skirt and jacket were a bit crisp
but my mum had lent me her old sparkly top
I thought I looked real class
Ross channelled Clint Eastwood chewing on his dad's cigar.
My cousin Ruth says she was there.

Five of us crammed into the Vauxhall Chevette
A dark night
A red light spiralling on the Ballygawley Road slowed us down
Checkpoints were common
Nothing to worry about
But this voice growled in a thick accent
dim yur feckin lights.
They blocked the road like a mob of black heifers
shrouded in protest blankets
and we were a flock of teenage lambs.

They wanted us out
they'd firebomb my dad's car
barricade the road
We believed John Lennon when he sang *Give Peace A Chance*
and I wasn't for getting out
it was ploutering it down
the rain would ruin my hair
I sunk the cuttie to the floor
spun the car round rallying
back down the road
Fists hammered the roof
the voice hollered
Come back here you wee hoor!

We all ducked expecting gun shots
rounding the second corner I almost wet myself laughing
We never thought to go home
We'd find another road over The Bann and on to Kildress Inn
We'd not waste a good night out for any old Blanketmen

Besides, the Catholic boy I'd read War and Peace for
was waiting and Fleetwood Mac were singing *Go Your Own Way*
Monday Morning we'd be back to school
and what a grand story we'd tell our friends.
None of us ever said anything to our parents
Sure there was no harm done no one had died

JEANETTE BURTON

Outstanding

After a while, when your working life
consists of formal observations, informal
observations, peer observations, learning
walks, Ofsted inspections, subject showcases,
deep dives, you feel like you are on your driving
test every single day, someone always
by your side, ready at any moment, but never
the one you expect, to slap the windscreen
with a clipboard, sending you into existential
despair and a fudged emergency stop.
It's like being under constant surveillance,
wearing a wire, knowing that there's a van
parked up down a road somewhere, blacked out
windows, satellite paraphernalia on the roof,
two members of the senior leadership team
tapping their earpieces, scribbling down
something desperately important about your
lesson objectives. And it's not just the classroom.
Oh no, they tail you all the way back home,
long range cameras snapping every movement,
evidence that health and safety is at the forefront
of your mind when you enter the house: trip
hazards minimised, wall displays maintained,
optimum temperature, electronic equipment
in full working order. And then your own kids,
are they on task? Can you chart their learning
progress from the day they came screaming
into this world to their current refusal to go to bed
at a reasonable hour? Tea must meet standards
1.a, 2.c, 4.e, nutritious, bland, no foreign cuisine,
but also, all singing, all dancing, and don't forget
to stop the fun between main and dessert,
check if fish, chips and beans has made a lasting
impression. Nowhere is off limits, not even
the bathroom or the bedroom. And when you climb
into bed, snuggle with your partner, sex is the plenary.
You tell yourself to make it measurable, because
no one wants requires improvement, or heaven forbid,

satisfactory.

LYDIA MACPHERSON

Franconia Notch

'On this site on the night of September 19-20, 1961, Betty and Barney Hill experienced a close encounter with an unidentified flying object and two hours of lost time while driving south from Canada. This was the first widely reported UFO abduction in the United States.'

The lake was slowing to ice at the shore.
The town, end-of-season, wanting rid
of strangers, turning its face, hunkering down.
We drove miles of moose-less highways,
past mossy trailer parks, Dunkin Donuts
like waystations en route to Mars.

On the third day we made Franconia Notch.
Cold peeled our hands, we swept snow
from the signboard, learnt
of the Barney and Betty Hill Incident.
As we were busy being born,
these lovers lost and found themselves.

Barney and Betty, in their '57 Chevy,
in the pine-edged layby. Here's Delsey
the dog sniffing neon-tinted dark,
here, 'eight to eleven humanoids'
in 'glossy black uniforms'.
The couple wake thirty miles south,
clothes torn, hours taken, sensing
their bodies had been explored;
the Chevy's roof is pocked with circles,
Delsey gone to the unknown.
Betty draws a star chart
whose centre is Zeta Reticuli.

The Notch was thrilling to their frequency:
the shift of air something more than
the wind funnelling down from Canada.
Later, warm at the motel on the interstate,
our touch was strange to each other,
as if we had an extra sense to learn,
as if we had made landfall in a new country.

Roman Coin Found at Top Withens

Were you marching up the ridge from Stanbury to Colne,
aiming for Vindolanda in that cold border land?

Or were you a woman, heading over the hill to Halifax
hoping to sell your homespun or buy some grain?

We cannot know, but, traveller, how I want you
to have been content in your long-ago life:

not homesick, not heartworn but happy
under this high blue dome of summer

with my skylarks' and curlews' ancestors
singing to you, the bilberries ripe,

a tree for shade and the warm grass
to take your rest on.

Exhibit

Exhibit 7.1: digital image, dated 2024.
Created using crude technology, pre-AI.
A bumblebee, probably *bombus monticola,* the bilberry bumblebee.
Extinct by 2032.

GRAHAM MORT

Fever

Young martins on the wire
out from their nest-fever
waiting to be fed in black
and white outfits in late summer
their parents raising one last brood
before the flight south.

They're over the bay like bats at dusk
flickering after-images of themselves
then at dawn they're angels
of sky's depth or soutaned
priests touching down
to bless their flock.

That fleeting communion
of bodily hunger
the thirst of the spirit sated
in sky burnished by wings
the globe's magnetic poles pulling
them over continents.

Each iteration of home
dawns as longing
the sky radioactive
the air pulsing with heat
with distance upon distance
future upon future.

Mountains heat thermals
to guide them so they'll return
whenever spring's in spate
a few survivors winging
through the smoke of ruined cities
the dust to dust of human hate.

Insomnia

Childhood is for adults
who need to sleep now
who had to be grown-ups
when they were children
listening for voices all night
watching the moon carving
frost patterns on windows
hearing the fury
of telephone wires sobbing
as the handset downstairs
slept in its cradle
the shriek of owls
answering the shriek of owls
cats copulating
their love a kind of rage
the low buzz of voices
persisting
sawing the house down
into the black waters
of insomnia
dark as the eye
of a woman stuffing
bedsheets into her mouth
at fist flurries
so the children wouldn't
couldn't but they did
of course they did
hear her bruises
blossoming
to bouquets.

REBECCA ALTHAUS

I Can't Write About Beauty

without mentioning my mother's neck
lifts – the first at seventy-two, the second
at eighty, or Dr Ian, member of the British College
of Aesthetic Medicine, who looks after my sister's
skin, or the way my friend paints her nails
because her husband thinks it enhances her
attractiveness, and how the real, unspoken,
reason I've given up cigarettes are the grooves
deepening above my upper lip.

I can't write about beauty without
mentioning my mother's guilt for everything
she would have done differently, or my sister's
messy interior held in by perfect brittleness,
or my friend's easy humour and knowing
wink to our feminist history in the generosity
she shows her man, or my loneliness
to feel the tentative then harder
press of another's lips on mine.

In a Field at Midsummer

Lying in a froth of Lady's Bedstraw in a field
at Bodrifty I'm learning to do nothing. I'm learning
to lie in this lady's soft bed, in this field, in today's
hot sun and ignore my mind's demanding voice.

Pleasure is sniffing me out, sniffing out my longings,
the ones I've forgotten. The easy ground, the rising
scent of honey and mown hay, her tiny yellow flowers
pressed up against my cheeks, making me

remember what I'm trying to move on from. I'm down
in the grasses, detonating seeds, my eyes
spilling over, my heart booming, rolling,
fresh cut on this longest day.

CLIFF YATES

Bus to Cirencester

12.10 outside the hospital, high summer
and we go upstairs like we usually do
at the front with our feet up like a couple
of kids, the trees in full leaf whipping
the windows, like driving through a forest.

It's a habit since taking up the guitar,
randomly allocating instruments to strangers
to form an imaginary band; that bloke
across the aisle in the orange t-shirt—drums.

The Daglingworth turn off, we can't
pass here without thinking of David,
staying with him in Vienna.
How old would he be now?

In Cirencester we'll head for the cafe
in the Corn Hall, our table with the drawer
mysteriously full of old teapot lids,
and Oxfam where one time I found
the Hart Crane biography *Voyager*.
    Bequeath us to no earthly shore

But that's the future and we're not
there yet, we're only arriving.
'Shall I wake up the bass player?'
He's been like that since Charlton Kings
holding onto his shopping trolley,
head on his hands. 'No,' she says
without missing a beat, 'let him sleep.'

Three Dog Night

Three Dog Night on my cassette player
waiting for my girlfriend, leaning
on the wall of the corner shop.
I used to deliver papers here,
Shredded Wheat before I set out,
egg on toast when I got back home
then off to school on my bike.
Newspapers, house numbers pencilled on,
*Woman's Realm, Titbits, The People's
Friend* (same cover, different cover),
The Beano, a *Parade* discreetly
folded in Monday's *Daily Mail* (number 91).
Newsprint on my fingers, the smell
of newspaper, the weight of the bag
on my shoulder, Three Dog Night
on my cassette player, music wherever I want.
This is the future and I am in it.

LINDA FORD

Bottle

We're upstairs on the bus, I'm reading
Ferlinghetti's *San Francisco Poems*
that I found in Oxfam and my head
is in San Francisco when an energy drink
bottle rattles its way from the back
—the girls behind us laugh—
and parks under our seat
I give it a kick and next
thing it's on the stairs
how'd it get there?
and sure enough next time
we brake it's off down, two,
three steps at a time we should
give it a round of applause
send it on its way like
you remember Italian airline
passengers applauding
in the 1970s when the pilot lands.
Well you can bet your life that bottle's not
climbing back up.

Renaissance

If doubts were raised about the new
damp course, an insidious stain emanating
from the chimney breast might settle the argument.
It's hardly the Turin Shroud, but a watermark
resembling a cow has appeared on the plasterwork.
Aside from the head and neck, a butcher might describe
the parts on display as chuck, brisket, and shank.
The left ear looks like it's tagged, and the right
appears to repel a troublesome fly.
Perhaps it's a Friesian making her way to the gate at milking
time, or, God forbid, on route to the abattoir.
Either way, I've become quite attached to this piece
of bovine art, which gradually reveals more of itself
like a slowly developing photograph.

ANGELA NEENAN

First symptoms

These days, receptionists want to know
your entire life story before they'll
book you in.

I can taste custard in my left eye,
I tell the woman at the end of the phone.
She gives me the locum 9.45.

It's my left eye, I tell him. Look.

I tip my head back, mouth full of teeth *aaarghh*.
Take off your blouse, he says gravely.
That's a bit forward, I think,

doing it anyway. My fingers have never
undone buttons before. The air bites my
shoulders. This may well hurt,

he says, making a bird from his graceful hands
swooping and diving at my sternum.
My own bird flaps miserably, utterly

outflanked. His eyes are jewel boxes.
This is much more serious than either of us thought,
he says.

MARION NEW

Green

Waking after a stolen sleep
I had green vision.

I could hear the Look North
weather forecast – rain –

the post thumping onto the floor
and a helicopter overhead.

Gradually the green dissipated
back to red velvet curtains,

a white orchid and an orange
and brown crocheted blanket.

MATTHEW PAUL

Green Tomato Chutney

Bamboo canes list, like yacht masts, beneath these hordes
    of thickset, snot-green lads, as comical as gourds,

growing still, but reluctant to redden, unlike smaller sistren
    and brethren that I, glory hunter, prise off the vine.

Lyn did all the staking and cultivating while I just sat on my
    iron chair, soaking up rays, admiring her industry.

This morning, I'll simmer green whoppers, with onion, salt,
    pepper, garlic, tart apples from a neighbour's glut,

sultanas, demerara, white wine vinegar, turmeric, cinnamon,
    ginger and cumin; till, around my wooden spoon,

the brown gunk thickens, like grief; maintaining the family
    tradition of brewing preserves: Granddad's jellies;

Mum's marmalades and jams—greengage the best, conjured
    out of the fruit from Orpington Maureen's orchard.

To Me, to You

To my brother, I WhatsApp
a link to a *Guardian* feature
marking the fiftieth anniversary
of *Autobahn*. He answers
in the middle of the night,
from Singapore, with pictures
of the Imperial Palace in Kyoto
and Todaji Buddhist temple in Nara.
At breakfast, I ask how his mastery
of Japanese is progressing. 'Well,'
he replies, 'I can manage ordering
in restaurants and buying stuff,
straightforward chat. It's tricky
reaching the next level.'

'Excellent,' I say.

I daren't tell him the breaking news
from Rotherham: frozen pipes, a rat
infestation and my angst about
almost everything. This morning,
the rat catcher will return, snow
permitting, to repeat the bombshell
that he's been here previously, not
long before we came. He'll show me
photos of 'reyt bigguns', trapped
in another customer's home,
explain how rats follow pheromones,
and at last shine a torch for checking,
behind kickboards in the kitchen,
the fruits, or otherwise, of his poison.

POETS I GO BACK TO

For this issue **Jane Draycott** and **Kate Potts** choose the poets who have made a difference to their own writing

JANE DRAYCOTT

    Whenever I am visiting my mother
    I feel I am turning into Emily Brontë,

    my lonely life around me like a moor,
    my ungainly body stumping over the mud flats with a look of transformation
    that dies when I come in the kitchen door.
    What meat is it, Emily, we need?
        (from 'The Glass Essay', Anne Carson, *Glass, Irony and God*, New Directions Publishing, 1996)

I've never very successfully managed a long poem but would love to be able to. To live for a sustained imaginative time taken up and entangled in something larger than the shortish lyric still feels like the Holy Grail, and **Anne Carson** has always seemed the model of that to me. Her work continuously demonstrates an ambition – a necessity – to get beyond the 'I' who sits down to write, finding the way fast to a space much bigger than the initial writing self, where beyond also in some way includes before, and as much elsewhere as any given starting-ground. Her 1995 long poem 'The Glass Essay', a 44-page narration at the end of a love affair via – amongst other things – a meditation on the life of Emily Brontë, has always felt like a talisman of that achievement. The 'Essay' of Carson's title is a reminder of the sort of enterprise a long poem – perhaps any poem – can be: an *attempt* at doing exploratory justice to something asking urgently to be started on and 'assayed' – tested for its weight and scope, breadth and depth. All of Carson's work provides inspiration like this but there's something particularly beautiful in the clarity of 'The Glass Essay', not least her consummate sense of how psychological scene and multiple association work together:

    ... early this morning while mother slept

    and I was downstairs reading the part in
        Wuthering Heights
    where Heathcliff clings at the lattice in the
        storm sobbing
    Come in! Come in! To the ghost of his heart's darling

    I fell on my knees on the rug and sobbed too.
    She knows how to hang puppies,
    that Emily.

That ever-expansive relation between experience and the imagination that Carson seems so brilliantly able to mine is probably what has also always drawn me to **Moniza Alvi**'s wonderfully poised and often beautifully surreal work. My first encounter with the brilliant 'I would like to be a dot in a painting by Miro' (1993), was the beginning of a long-term admiration for the fantastic balance she achieves between uncertainty and certainty, between strangeness and understanding:

    I'll never make out what's going on
    around me, and that's the joy of it.
    .../...
    A child's adventure.
    And nothing in this tawny sky
    can get too close, or move too far away.
        (from *Split World: Poems 1990-2005*, Bloodaxe Books 2008)

All of Carson's work provides inspiration like this but there's something particularly beautiful in the clarity of 'The Glass Essay'...

Elsewhere across all her collections the same edgy, often touching, wryness and delicately-judged distance appear again and again:

> She is not the woman I met.
> She never was.
> The cock crows,
> The dawn whitens.
> It appeals to me that this is so
> ('After Escher', from *How the Stone Found Its Voice*, 2005)

It's there also in *Homesick for the Earth,* her superb 2011 versions of the work of the surrealist Jules Supervielle, a collection that I found really illuminating and inspiring when I was working on translations of Supervielle's great friend Henri Michaux.

Like others in this series I'm sure, I can't go without mentioning the unmatchable **Michael Donaghy**, whose work sings unforgettably in the mind long after listening to any of the recordings of his performances. I first heard his reading of his sonnet 'Southwesternmost' when Ian McMillan played it on 'The Verb' (BBCR4) the day after Donaghy died in 2004, and that recording has become a personal touchstone ever since. An elegy for his mother, it travels across an astonishingly moving montage of sound and image and thought, his mind's eye simultaneous with his musician's ear, searching and mapping with typical Donaghy subtlety and grace. Ignited by the opening conceit of a compass 'tooled for reckoning by time', the poem opens up a kaleidescope of south-western quadrant imagery ('the lower left edge of this chart,/ the damaged chamber of my mother's heart') that builds and coalesces towards its echoing final half-rhyme:

> I can almost hear it now and hold its shape,
> the famine song she's humming in my sleep.
> (from *Safest,* Picador 2005)

Finally, to look forward as much as back, there's the wonderfully energising work of **Harry Man**, whose debut 2024 collection *Popular Song* (Nine Arches) has had me going back to it often since it first appeared, plugging into the battery re-charge of his seriously playful poetics. It's a collection of real originality, scattered with frequent moments of pathos in its boundless engagement with language – marvelling and transformative, driven by curiosity and invention:

> So I talked into the packaging
> of the American Inspired Loaded Chicken Wings
> as if it would answer me
> and I saw the naked red earth.
> ... / ...
> At the end of the night shift
> I swim to beyond the limit
> of the terrazzo archipelagos
> but like so many daydreams
> that product is currently unavailable.
> ('Naked as a Pork Loin Steak in a Poppy Field,
> I Consider a Horse from the Future')

And the aesthetic he's giving searching life to isn't contained only in his own page-poems. It's also in his digital/visual poetic experiments as well as in his translation work, notably in his collaborations with the Norwegian poet Endre Ruset, *Utøya Therafter: Poems in Memory of the 2011 Norway Attacks* and *Noriaki*, poems in tribute to the legendary ski-jumper Noriaki Kasai.

If you're not already reading Harry Man, discover him on Instagram and other platforms or at www.manmadebooks.

It's a collection of real originality, scattered with frequent moments of pathos in its boundless engagement with language ...

The Poets

Moniza Alvi, *Split World: Poems 1990-2005*, Bloodaxe Books 2008

Jules Supervielle and Moniza Alvi, *Homesick for the Earth: Selected Poems*, Bloodaxe Books 2011

Anne Carson, *Glass, Irony and God*, New Directions Publishing 1996

Michael Donaghy, *Safest*, Picador 2005

Harry Man, *Popular Song*, Nine Arches Press 2024

KATE POTTS

I first discovered Anne Carson's work in Streatham Library in the early 2000s. I was not long out of university, working in a mind-numbing data entry job and wondering if my working life would ever engage my mind in ways that felt genuinely meaningful or creative. Fiona Benson has talked about the poets she most admires as 'permission-givers'. Reading Anne Carson's *Autobiography of Red* reshaped my ideas of what poetry could be and do, as well as opening up my sense of my own potential creative life. *Autobiography of Red*, described as 'A Novel in Verse', remakes the story of the red winged monster Geryon who, in ancient Greek mythology, was killed by demi-god Herakles as one of his labours. Drawing on fragments from the work of ancient Greek poet Stesichoros, Carson shifts Geryon from monstrous, peripheral victim to the heart of the story. Stesichorus, we're told, who 'came after Homer and before Gertrude Stein', shifted away from standard Homeric epithets. The Iliad and the Odyssey are thick with these epithets: formulaic, repeatedly used adjectives or phrases communicating attributes thought to be characteristic of particular people or things, for example: 'wine-dark sea', 'swift-footed Achilles', 'death-dealing spear'. The use of these prefabricated groupings in Homer is thought to originate in the mnemonic, formulaic building blocks of epic narratives passed on by spoken word alone, and in the constraints of dactylic hexameter metre. Stesichorus, according to Carson, introduced a radical new approach to description:

> Stesichorus released being. All the substances in the world went floating up. Suddenly there was nothing to interfere with horses being hollow hooved. Or a river being root silver. Or a child bruiseless.

In Carson's version of the story, awkward contemporary teenage monster Geryon falls in love with older, more confident Herakles. The violence of the encounter as originally told in Greek mythology is recast and reconfigured in the sexual power dynamics of the relationship.

> Geryon was amazed at himself. He saw Herakles just
> about every day now.
> The instant of nature
> forming between them drained every drop from the
> walls of his life
> leaving behind just ghosts
> rustling like an old map. He had nothing to say to
> anyone. He felt loose and shiny.
> He burned in the presence of his mother.

In the pulsing of the 47 poems' alternating long and short lines there is sharp and tender description of domestic life, as well as discussion of photography, autobiography, philosophy, volcanoes, Emily Dickinson, the possibilities and limits of language – as well as what it might mean to be a red monster with wings. There's whimsy and wry comedy, and also utter seriousness. *Autobiography of Red* was the perfect book for a bookish, dreamy twentysomething struggling with adulthood. But Carson's approach and preoccupations have continued to guide me as I've grown.

There are images in Carson's poetry that are so acutely crafted and emotionally stark I've committed them to memory without trying to: 'Coldness comes paring down from the moonbone in the sky' (from 'Father's Old Blue Cardigan'), 'Everything I know about love and its necessities/ I learned in that one moment/ when I found myself/ thrusting my little burning red backside like a baboon/ at a man who no longer cherished me' ('The Glass Essay') … As well as this direct, more traditionally lyric mode, there are also references and allusions to – and sometimes inclusions of – other voices, texts and artworks. In *Nox*, Carson's elegy for her elusive dead brother, for example, we have Roman poet Catullus, the Latin/English dictionary, ancient Greek historian Herodotus, *The Bible* (Lazarus), and ancient Japanese poet Basho, alongside the speaker, her mother, her brother Michael, and Michael's partner. For me, this weaving together of everyday and

---

There are images in Carson's poetry that are so acutely crafted and emotionally stark I've committed them to memory without trying to …

domestic experience with more abstract, often bookish and learned modes of thinking and writing guides the reader, conversationally, through material that might otherwise feel exclusive or obscure. Carson also finds ways to open up the text and invite the reader into her process. *Nox*, for example, begins with Catullus' elegy 'Poem 101' in the original Latin. Throughout the rest of the book, on the left-hand side of the pages, are subtly doctored English dictionary definitions for the Latin words of 'Poem 101'. 'I never arrived at the translation I would have liked to do of Poem 101' the narrator tells us, towards the end of the book. On the opposite page is this meditation on translation:

> Human words have no main switch. But all those little kidnaps in the dark. And then the luminous, big, shivering, discandied, unrepentant, barking web of them that hangs in your mind when you turn back to the page you were trying to translate.

As with Stesichorus' refusal of Homeric epithets there's fascination and joy, throughout Carson's work, in reaching beyond or outside semantic meaning, and beyond more standard and familiar structures and modes of understanding. *Autobiography of Red* is 'A Novel in Verse'. *The Beauty of The Husband* is labelled 'A Fictional Essay in 29 Tangos'. *Float* is 'A collection of twenty-two chapbooks whose order is unfixed and whose topics are various'. The books tend to deny and refuse easy categorisation, juxtaposing and colliding different registers, time periods, genres and forms.

The struggle to use form – its muscle and movement – to shape, hone and contain my writing has been central to my work. From very early on, influenced by Dylan Thomas, I've wanted to write a piece of work with multiple voices in dialogue, to create a sense of community on the page. I've tried and failed to write a narrative sequence for voices, and a radio play.

In 2021 I became a solo parent and moved from Hackney in London to Stroud in Gloucestershire. The impact of this in my working and creative life has been seismic, and I'm still readjusting. These days my reading is fragmentary, fitted into snatched moments, jammed up against or pressed into service of care for my child and the need to provide for us both. And yet, at the living-room table, I've been able to forge new ways of writing and making new work. I've woven together material from original interviews with prose essay fragments, dramatic monologues, and my own more straightforwardly 'personal' poems to create *Pretenders*, a book about imposter feelings, pretence and identity that feels, for once, cohesive and fully realised. Twenty years or so after I first discovered Anne Carson's work I'm learning, finally, that I can weld and weave together a form that suits what I'm making, rather than pouring it – or my creative life – into a predetermined shape.

The Poets

Anne Carson, *Autobiography of Red*, Jonathan Cape, 1999

Anne Carson, *Nox*, New Directions Publishing, 2009

Anne Carson, *Float*, Jonathan Cape, 2016

As with Stesichorus' refusal of Homeric epithets there's fascination and joy, throughout Carson's work, in reaching beyond or outside semantic meaning ...

About the Authors

Jane Draycott's latest collection is *The Kingdom* (2022), her sixth publication with Carcanet Press. Her most recent translation work, *Storms Under the Skin: poems of Henri Michaux 1927-54*, is published by Two Rivers Press. In 2023 she was a recipient of a Society of Authors' Cholmondeley Award.

Kate Potts is a poet, lecturer, mentor and editor. Her latest book is *Pretenders* (Bloodaxe).

Michael Laskey at Eighty

We are delighted to publish this celebration, despite (or because of) how it will discomfit its subject. Thank you to Kay Laskey, Naomi Jaffa and Dean Parkin for reminding us of *The North*'s previous feature, Michael Laskey at 60, and suggesting and helping put together this one.

Michael has published five books and three pamphlets, including a *Selected* and a *Very Selected Poems*. His *Collected Poems* will be published in the autumn. He co-founded the international Aldeburgh Poetry Festival in 1989 and directed it through its first decade, then becoming its Chair. He also founded and co-edited the poetry magazine *Smiths Knoll* through fifty much-loved issues. He published pamphlets under the *Smiths Knoll* imprint until 2016, and continues his work as an editor with The Garlic Press (which he established in 2003).

A long-term poetry activist, Michael was a founding member of the East Suffolk Poetry Workshop which has been meeting monthly for thirty years. A regular tutor for the Arvon Foundation, he currently leads Cut Loose monthly Saturday morning writing sessions – with Dean Parkin – originally at the arts centre in Halesworth, which have now migrated to online sessions on Zoom.

ANNE BERKELEY

'Michael's not a buildings person, he's a people person,' said Roy Blackman, when we asked whether Michael was joining the outing to Butley Priory. It was a *Smiths Knoll* weekend in the mid-90s, when the two editors of that legendary magazine ran workshops for subscribers.

They were a terrific double act. While Roy concerned himself with the structure, syntax, the internal logic of a poem, Michael would focus more on its emotional force, its beating heart.

Others will write about his scrupulous editing, and his own gracious, witty and humane poetry. I want to pay tribute to Michael's democratic, evangelical enthusiasm for the art.

Anyone who sent off their hopeful batch of poems will remember how they came back within a week, with encouraging comments – if you were very lucky they would even take one without amendments ('rare for us').

After one of these weekends I was invited to a masterclass. Michael managed to persuade me that the audience weren't there to see a bloodsport but because they were interested and wanted to learn. And Michael in the chair ensured that everything remained courteous and constructive.

And so I was inducted as a regular audience member of that joyous institution, The Aldeburgh Poetry Festival. As the years rolled by, we were introduced to just about every leading and newly emerging British poet you can think of, as well as international poets as varied as Les Murray, Philip Levine, Billy Collins, Anne Carson, Galway Kinnell … It's invidious to pick anyone out – there were so many. And what a difference it makes to hear the poet read their own poems. Their voice lodges in your head to bring it to their new work when you come across it. Every year we came home with a heavy book bag and fresh ideas.

LIZ BERRY

Michael was one of the first to publish me in *Smiths Knoll* (I wish I could remember the poem!) and I recall being so thrilled to get his little handwritten note of encouragement, a real way-post

His trademark poems – immaculately crafted, warm and eloquent – are at once a contemplation of the past and a love letter to the future.
– Craig Raine

on the journey. A wonderful poet and editor and a kind teacher. Wishing him the happiest of birthdays!

≈ PETER CARPENTER ≈

It was a poem about childhood, 'Another League', a young boy watching amateur football, sent in hope to Smith's Knoll, early in the 1990s. It came back to me, with an acceptance note, and some editorial advice, all of it spot on. The bit I remember most vividly is 'perhaps the pluperfect here?' My first encounter with Michael Laskey: warm and valuable advice; scholarship lightly borne; able, just like that, to sniff out any pseudery; an ear attuned to seek out and give a tweak to clunking rhythms, listening out for the 'music of what happens', as Heaney had it. I had met a master of his trade.

After that, Michael became the go-to person for an Arvon or Ty Newydd residential course; patient yet demanding, caring and generous, but never unrealistic, looking for the next draft, engaging with students we'd taken, pushing them because it mattered to him, conveying this urgency in all he did. 'Let's get on with this while we can'. Workshops that revealed a compendious knowledge of contemporary poetry, as well as an enviable reach back to the Metaphysical poets, the Romantics, tradition made vital in a rapid detour or a memorable allusion.

Michael's poetry readings on these courses were self-effacing (letting the words on the page do the job), no 'egotistical sublime', poems playful and daring, in control but pushing the boundaries. Minor miracles from the ordinary, the everyday. Moving, memorable. Arising from 'felt life': poems about marmalade, garlic, a bike, rain, sport's days, ironing, bonfires. And then a dramatic monologue like 'Driving Home', as read to students, their teachers and co-tutors, at Totleigh Barton in 2003. A poem that left all of us gaping at the reader's steady gaze as he calmly delivered that last sentence: 'Softly you close/the up-and-over garage door'.

≈ HELEN IVORY ≈

Michael is an inspirational tutor and a very safe pair of hands. When I was programming the Continuing Education creative writing courses at UEA, he was the first person I looked to to run an Advanced Poetry Diploma.

≈ NAOMI JAFFA ≈

I first met Michael in 1993 when he was on the interview panel for the part-time job of Suffolk's first Literature Development Worker. I gushed something about re-reading favourite classic novels and I remember being intensely disconcerted by the ironic incredulity of his 'you *re-read*?' response.

Despite a derisory knowledge of contemporary poetry, my new duties were to assist Michael run the Aldeburgh Poetry Festival which he'd co-founded in 1989. That first weekend in November 1993, I stepped through the back of a wardrobe to find myself in the Jubilee Hall, laughing and weeping, puzzling and marvelling at poets reading their own poems. I'd read English at Oxford and had no idea that literature could be so relevant and *alive*.

Radically and quite simply, Michael changed and underpinned the course of my life. For 22 years we worked closely together – productively, sometimes disputatiously, hospitably, always whole-heartedly – until the Festival ceased in 2015. Happily, our friendship has continued every year since.

They say 'when the student is ready, the teacher appears', and certainly I'd never have written or published my own poems without Michael's steadfast encouragement and editorial acuity. At our monthly workshop group (which I've been attending since the mid-1990s) it's his responses I value most. And being among the first to encounter a new Laskey poem is privilege, treat and education all in one.

'Gratitude' and 'love' are over-used and devalued words these days, but I don't know any better ones. Over and over again, for more than half my life,

Michael is an inspirational tutor and a very safe pair of hands.

Michael has made me feel like the best version of myself. I couldn't be more thankful to and for him.

⇋ HANNAH LOWE ⇌

Whenever I think of Michael Laskey, it's with envy. I imagine him in his house, which I imagine is somewhere near the sea where he swims, and that he has days devoted to poetry, and that when he does write poems – this is the really envious bit – they are always brilliant. I've carried his selected *The Man Alone* with me for years, because it's one of the few books I can drop into, read a poem, and immediately want to write a poem back to it. One of these is 'Ratatouille', a poem that stirs together its details (of food, books, home decor) and layers (social class, romance, youth, eroticism) so brilliantly, and carries a whole world in its final lines.

I can't quite believe Michael is 80. I was lucky enough to teach an Arvon with him five or so years ago, where we split the morning sessions in half; Michael teaching short, spritely poetry exercises which everyone loved, while I made them wade through different tricky poetic forms, which everyone endured.

Happy Birthday Michael. I have been a secret huge fan of you for years, and I'm glad now to out myself, in case you didn't know.

⇋ KATH McKAY ⇌

I met Michael at the 2000 Aldeburgh Poetry Festival after he gave me a lovely unsolicited quote for *Anyone Left Standing*. He turns up when you need him. Often, he would offer a lift from Saxmundham to Aldeburgh when I became a regular punter.

Later, he published my poems in *Smiths Knoll* magazine. Responses were quick, and rejections tempered by encouraging words.

Years later, out of the blue, he wrote '*Smiths Knoll* is closing down, and we have money left over to publish pamphlets by poets we like. We like you.' People underestimate how such words bolster you. Telling the Bees was the result, after I experienced Michael's laser sharp editing skills: 'Are you happy with that line?' 'What does that mean?' 'Is that the right word?' I responded to his directness because I know he lives to make poetry better. My second full collection, *Collision Forces* (Wrecking Ball), followed soon after, something which may not have happened without Michael's pamphlet.

After publishing a crime novel, I returned to poetry through attending workshops, including Cut Loose, run by Michael, and Dean Parkin. Using an eclectic range of poetry as springboards, interspersed with discussions about topics such as fried eggs, and stationery, from this mesh poetry emerges. I built towards another collection. Michael's Garlic Press published *Moving the Elephant* in 2024. I am very lucky to have had him as an editor. He has a way of making you think, done with humour and professionalism and a deceptive lightness that treats poetry as a dance.

Or a balancing act, like in his poem, 'Bike', where 'feet off the ground', the rider and the bicycle are 'keeping each other's balance', until the rider is 'clear of the wheel of myself'. His website image is him riding a bike. Ride on, Michael, ride on.

⇋ IAN McMILLAN ⇌

There are some people who hold the past, present and future of poetry in their hands, and Michael Laskey is one of them; for decades he has devoted his life to the placing of words on the page and in the air and he has continued to democratise and celebrate this most available of art forms by making it even more available to anyone who wants to experience it.

What really moves and inspires me about Michael is that, in turbulent and cruelly austere times, he understands that poetry is a way for us to make sense of a world that apparently makes no sense, and that a poem in a magazine or a discussion in a workshop or a moment at a reading can be something that can

I imagine him in his house, which I imagine is somewhere near the sea where he swims, and that he has days devoted to poetry ...

feed the soul for years to come.

Let's not forget that this devotion to poetry involves decades of sitting in rooms waiting for somebody to turn up, of sitting at dining room tables reading envelopes full of submissions as a deadline looms, of endlessly encouraging those who need encouragement and suggesting to others that the reshaping of that line might lead to a better stanza.

Thanks very much for all this, Michael: here's to the next 80 years!

ᕽ HELENA NELSON ᕽ

Just one word. He'll pop it into a line casually. A word like 'baffled', maybe, or 'perplexed'. But it's not just the word. It's the way his tone has prepared for its sound and shape. No fuss. Unobtrusively expert. Also his tenderness: he places it fondly, syllable by syllable – even when it has negative associations ('devastation', 'tarnished', 'interminably'). I don't know anyone else who cherishes language like this, so utterly, so devotedly. Whenever I read him, words he's invisibly earmarked leap out, and then I'm welling up. Why? Something to do with vividness, I think. Or mortality. Sometimes a bit of Laskey follows me round all day, and I can't not notice it ever again: 'fortitude', 'kerfuffle', 'fossicking'. Or unassuming terms like 'dollop', 'deft', 'humdrum'. There's that habit, too, of animating inanimate objects – an ironing-board, maybe, or chairs, curtains, a bicycle – even a bonfire. His bedside clock has a life of its own. But so do those words. In *Between Ourselves*, he says they're 'growing absent- / minded and will keep wandering off'. But they're safe enough in his poems. Alive and kicking for centuries, I'd say.

ᕽ NAOMI SHIHAB NYE ᕽ

Michael Laskey – will turn his face away from too much praise. But what a gracious, whimsical, endearing poet and soul! Energetic enough to create one of the truly unforgettable festivals, dear Aldeburgh, to welcome voices from everywhere, and to shape his own poems that restore our hearts to their sockets, our brains to their hope.

Thank you Michael Laskey for your marvellous being, your care, your tender gaze.

ᕽ DEAN PARKIN ᕽ

I heard about Michael Laskey before I met him. In the first days of my poetry adventures I summoned up the courage to attend an Arvon Course in May 1997, tutored by Roger McGough and Jo Shapcott at Lumb Bank.

During a wonderful week, I remember bemoaning the lack of any culture or poetry where I lived in Suffolk. Both Roger and Jo told me about a man called Michael Laskey who came from my part of the world. A lovely man, they said, who ran the Aldeburgh Poetry Festival and a great magazine called *Smiths Knoll*.

Later that year I got a poem published in *Smiths Knoll* and attended the Aldeburgh Poetry Festival and finally met Michael and his Festival assistant Naomi Jaffa who later became my partner in work and life.

I also started attending the workshop group which was led by Michael and his co-editor Roy Blackman. This really did form the foundations of what became my life as poet, and I worked with Michael and Naomi at the Festival for fifteen years until it ceased in 2015.

Michael quickly became my hero, mentor and friend. That we've known each other for almost 30 years now is astonishing. That Michael is 80 and still fiercely passionate about poems – reading, writing and editing them – was only ever to be expected and deserves to celebrated. It's the Laskey zeal and the sharp editorial eye that I treasure. He also has the best laugh too, head back and full-hearted guffaw, and we're still laughing whenever we get together for our next poetry adventures. As he says, it's the most fun.

That Michael is 80 and still fiercely passionate about poems – reading, writing and editing them – was only ever to be expected and deserves to celebrated.

STEPHEN PAYNE

I was a very lucky learner poet. Late in 2009, I received a hand-written letter from Michael inviting me to be the *Smiths Knoll* mentee. Michael is a great teacher as well as a great poet, and for the same reason: how brilliantly he blends rigour and generosity. Michael taught me that every phrase, every word is an opportunity to make a poem special. One of the best reviews I received for 'Pattern Beyond Chance' complimented a particular verb in one poem. The poem dated from my year learning with Michael, and the verb in question was Michael's suggestion.

Michael's poem 'Laughter' (from *Between Ourselves*) does not require any elucidation from me, though I learn something every time I read it. I simply want to note the insightful, alliterative expression "warming to oneself / for one's wit". The use of "one" is surprisingly formal within such a natural register, but perfectly appropriate for that remoteness of the self-critic, the slight dissatisfaction with his personality that even a contented man might sometimes feel. It's a poem, surely, about Michael's conversations with his wife Kay, but I like to imagine Michael warming to himself as he made another witty suggestion for one of my poems, brightening the day for both of us.

SHEENAGH PUGH

I met Michael at Aldeburgh and came away with his book *Thinking of Happiness*. There was a poem in it called "Firelighters", about a woman whose marriage has ended and who is learning to cope with everyday jobs her husband used to do. It was a very useful poem for students, because it was all concrete, no abstracts, showing the change in the woman via what she does and how she does it. So I used it a lot in workshops. One day, when we'd just been reading it, one of my students remarked. "That's my mum". I thought at first he was being metaphorical, that his mother had had this same experience, but no, it turned out she knew Michael and it was in fact her experience that had inspired the poem. It was the perfect answer to those students who sometimes wondered what poetry had to do with real life and I think it helped convince them that seemingly commonplace aspects of real life are just waiting to be transmuted into poetry. Best wishes to Michael for many more birthdays.

CHRISTOPHER REID

Even before I got to know Michael as an excellent poet and all-round mensch, I admired him for his performances at the Aldeburgh Poetry Festival. Quite simply, he was, in that context, the best introducer of poets at readings that I have ever heard. It was not just that he was well-prepared, had read the work of the poet in question thoroughly and critically, or could find trenchant and illuminating phrases by which to sum up that work and make it approachable to listeners. Above and beyond all that, it was the warm, earnest and gracious manner in which he fulfilled this function that made one listen, first to the introduction, then to the poet's reading, with a buoyed-up attentiveness that was rare. There may, too, have been a touch of schoolmasterly sternness about it, as if Michael were saying to the audience, 'I've done my job, now you do yours. This is a serious business. Listen carefully!' Of course we listened carefully.

PHILIP RUSH

It is a bit of a cliché to say that poems can make the ordinary extraordinary; what Michael's poems do, more often than not, I think, is to celebrate the ordinary simply by recording it, and in ordinary language. This is a dangerous game to play and it is to Michael's credit that he pulls it off so well. The poems end with humble flourishes. "Softly you close/ the up-and-over garage door." "… head down, holding the music", "a whole/ day of snow nobody's trodden." They deceive, of course. The journey itself is "up and over". How

It is a bit of a cliché to say that poems can make the ordinary extraordinary; what Michael's poems do, more often than not, I think, is to celebrate the ordinary simply by recording it …

can anyone "hold" music? With a moment of stillness such as the pianist exemplifies?

The other day I found myself looking over some of my old poems. The ones that had been included in *Smiths Knoll* remain fringed with joy. Michael's personal support has been a blessing. In getting my recent book through the press (Camera Obscura), his work and help were generous and exemplary.

Happy Birthday, Michael, and thank you.

JACQUELINE SAPHRA

In the early 2000s I would often go to the Poetry Library in the Southbank Centre to browse the magazines. I always looked for *Smiths Knoll*. Here were engaging, emotionally connective, crafted poems. *Smiths Knoll* became my first port of call when I was submitting new poems, largely because I felt it was a natural home for my work but partly because the turn-around was astonishingly quick. Whereas some magazines could take up to a year to respond, Michael would come back within three or four days. In my case it was invariably a 'no, but …' and occasionally 'we loved it but …' followed by a paragraph of analysis and yes, praise. These were rejections that felt both useful and affirming. After years of trying, however, I finally achieved my dream although I almost fainted when I opened the envelope fully expecting the usual warm rejection and found an acceptance. I didn't have to implement his suggested changes, Michael told me in characteristically generous style – the poem was in either way. But of course I did pay attention and the poem was better for it. Devastatingly, this gem of a magazine was closed very soon after that, so I never had a chance to try again. But it was a beautiful endeavour, Michael Laskey was its presiding spirit and I learnt so much from him. I'm tempted to say they broke the mould when they made him, but that's a dead metaphor I daresay he wouldn't appreciate. They don't make editors like that any more.

PAUL STEPHENSON

Michael taught me so much about the poetic line when I was starting to send out, and about the ordering of ideas in narrative poems. I would submit to *Smiths Knoll*, those brown envelopes coming back within 3-4 days, always hoping to feel the envelope thinner, a poem accepted. I was told once that he writes slowly, perfecting each line before proceeding to the next one, but I am not sure whether to believe that and wonder if he ever goes in for overall edits of the whole. His landmark collection *Permission to Breathe* (Smith|Doorstop 2004) came out 20 years ago and did what it said, giving me a way forwards in my writing. I was so privileged to be accepted onto the Aldeburgh Eight with him and Peter Sansom as tutors at Bruisyard Hall, to have a pass for the incredible Aldeburgh Poetry Festival at Snape, and even Naomi popped in for some writing exercises that year. In my time helping programme Poetry in Aldeburgh, it has been a joy to have events showcasing Garlic Press and hear the wonderful Suffolk poets he has encouraged and published. Always thrilled to see Michael in Aldeburgh, beret or no beret, and to hear him read his poems so beautifully. I am so grateful for his early influence, the attention to my poems, and encouragement he has given.

ALICIA STUBBERSFIELD

Twenty-five years ago Michael drove Neil Rollinson, Angela McSeveney and me around Suffolk for a week. Those who know Michael's driving might consider that quite an adventure but we had a wonderful time on that Aldeburgh Poetry Festival Tour. We read at nine events and after each of our readings (all twenty-seven of them) Michael had something constructive, rigorous but kind to say about our performance. I still hear his voice when I read my work to an audience, or I'm listening to another poet – any poets reading this make sure you have a set list, stick to it and don't go over time!

I'm tempted to say they broke the mould when they made him, but that's a dead metaphor I daresay he wouldn't appreciate.

That was my first visit to Aldeburgh Poetry Festival and I went every year after that. Founded by Michael, the warm, welcoming atmosphere and creation of a poetry community free of rivalries and cynicism was absolutely him.

There's no-one in the poetry world like Michael. No-one with his generosity, his authentic love of poetry and his enthusiasm for encouraging the poetry of others. His tutorials, on an Arvon Schools Course I tutored with him, were a joy. At the point where any other tutor would have shut things down, Michael said something like 'and what about this word here…' and the conversation with the teenage girl or boy would begin again. To be in one of his workshops is to feel the same intense pleasure we felt when we began to write poems. To read Michael's own poetry is to feel a sense of wonder at his ability to create accessible poems, often about everyday things or experiences, that are beautifully crafted and have that controlled ambiguity found only in the best writing. Michael's humanity and self-deprecating humour give hope and delight to all of us lucky enough to know and love him.

⇒ EMILY WILLS ⇐

I love Michael's poems for their clarity, how they hold their truth lightly, and for the way they make such skill appear easy. It's impossible to choose favourites, but the poems I'm thinking of now are 'Home Movies', 'Between Ourselves', and the unforgettable self-portrait 'Nightingales'. I have 'The Last Swim' by heart, having read it at my mother's funeral where it was quite simply perfect.

Thank you, Michael, for the brilliant *Smiths Knoll*. And for your extraordinary generosity in commenting on submissions, always spot-on. Thank you for Aldeburgh Poetry Festival, that ear-opening invigorating buzz of a weekend. I'm still in awe at the vision and sheer work of creating and sustaining it. Special mention to those mass workshops, hordes of us crammed in, surprising ourselves with high-speed and surprisingly half-decent drafts of poems thanks to Michael's wizardry and calm.

And now we have Cut Loose online, with the incomparable pairing of Dean and Michael, hilarious and inspiring. Another poetry treat you've brought us. Happy birthday Michael! May you go on swimming.

⇒ ANTHONY WILSON ⇐

Michael Laskey's listening. Connie Bensley and I had given a reading at the Peter Pears Gallery in Aldeburgh and were now being driven by Michael through dark Suffolk lanes to drop Connie off at her digs. If memory serves, it was raining and Michael had to swerve to avoid hitting a fox. This did nothing to stop the torrent of words which at that moment were pouring from him on poetry, poets, art, music – and the wretched weather.

In something of a fight-or-flight reverie, which reminds me now of how I spent most of my time at school, I seemed to join him midway through his theme, alerted, as at school, by mention of my name: '… but I have to say to you, Anthony, that I don't really want to hear that your monologues are 'amalgams', as you put it, of different people, I want to know that they are *one* person … .' Suddenly awake and trying to find something to say about nearly killing the fox, it dawned on me that Michael was reporting back words I had used not an hour earlier in introduction to one of my poems. Words I had not planned on saying, words I found myself saying to fill the space, words I now knew (and knew then) were not true. Like a human lie detector, Michael had picked this up. I knew it was useless to argue with him.

In my experience, feedback like this, honest feedback that is not designed to crush you but help you do better next time, in whatever sphere, let alone planet poetry, is rare. Difficult to hear, more difficult still to practise, he set me a standard for transparency. Do I meet it? Somewhere in the darkness, I can feel him listening.

There's no-one in the poetry world like Michael. No-one with his generosity, his authentic love of poetry and his enthusiasm for encouraging the poetry of others.

⇋ TAMAR YOSELOFF ⇋

Over the years, Michael Laskey has created a vital and important hub for poetry in his home county of Suffolk, championing local and UK writers in the pages of the wonderful *Smiths Knoll* magazine, which he edited with Roy Blackman, and then through his Garlic Press, a small but mighty independent publisher. His popular writing workshops have inspired a whole generation of new voices, many of whom found their way to the Aldeburgh Poetry Festival, which he founded and kept running with Naomi Jaffa and Dean Parkin for 25 years, bringing the most significant and engaging poets – national and international – to the Suffolk coast. The current iteration of the poetry festival is incredibly indebted to him, and his tireless (but always generous) spirit – we wouldn't be here, continuing the tradition of poetry by the sea, without him – he's still cutting a dash in his trademark beret.

Somewhere in the darkness, I can feel him listening.

Laskey & Son Present

Thinking of Happiness Etc

Michael and Jack's Unique Theatre Collaboration
With Music, Poetry, Dance, Film + Friends

September
Saturday 13th @ 4pm
Sunday 14th @ 7:30pm

Jubilee Hall,
Crabbe Street,
Aldeburgh,
Suffolk

PLEASE HELP BRING THIS SHOW TO LIFE:

SEARCH 'CROWDFUNDER THINKING OF HAPPINESS ETC.'

More info and tickets available here:
https://aldeburghjubileehall.co.uk/

MICHAEL LASKEY

Firelighters
For Lesley

Soon after he left you, another first:
entering the cold husk of the house
with two tired children you know the worst
has happened. The Parkray has gone out

and find yourself kneeling without thinking
without faith before the boiler,
riddling briskly, cinders and clinker
cleared, the grate a waiting void

which he'd have filled with his unhurried
origami, a fan of spills
pinched round compact coils and buried
under kindling, chips of coal.

Always miraculous that phoenix,
now extinguished. But all you need's
to hand: a screwed-up man-size Kleenex,
a firelighter, some sticks and a hod

of coal to feed a single match.
Nothing to it. You lift the flap
for draught, adjust the thermostat
and feel warmth slowly welling up.

The Clothes-peg

How it had happened they neither of them knew
but it only got worse. He hated the blank
blue ice of his stare and she couldn't bear
her thin voice telling him to turn
down the TV please, to stop diddling
with that clothes-peg, which without thinking he
clipped to the hem of her cardigan hanging
over the newel post as he mooched past.
It was Margaret at work who pointed it out
and all day it kept on taking her hand
by surprise, a bump in her cardigan pocket.
So naturally closing his old Noah's Ark
curtains that evening she pegged them together.
A few mornings later it waylaid her
inside her shoe. She snapped it on the end
of his toothbrush handle, so it wouldn't pull through
the holder, and found it next clipping the ear
of Humph, her venerable bear. For him she left it
dangling in the dark from the plastic light pull
in the bathroom, where he lit on the pot
of Paracetamol and dibbled it in.
It felt like a biro caught in his train pass
as he brought it out to show the guard,
and tugging a Kleenex out of the box
she spluttered at the clatter, but said nothing,
just hung it from the lining inside his tie
ready for the morning. And now the drizzle starts
as she's driving to work, she laughs out loud -
lifted by it skimming back and forth
riding on the stalk of the wiper blade.

Bike

You, who have borne three sons
of mine, still bear my weight
routinely, transporting me.
An odd pair: your classic spare
lines – elbows, bony frame –
and me, bearlike, cumbersome,
nosing tangled coils of air
you cut through with your pure
purposeful geometry.
With you it's feet off the ground,
a feat passing unremarked
though in full public view.
Keeping each other's balance.
Our talk slow recurrent clicks,
companionable creaks.
Through you I've come to know
winds inside out and raw
weather ignored before;
and nuances of slopes,
the moving earth, green tracks
for blackberries and sloes
for gin, for jam: the tug
and tang of fruit pulling me
clear of the wheel of myself.

Weighing the Present

I didn't believe it for a minute
but turning the corner at the lights
saw him waiting on the opposite pavement
outside A1 Discounts to cross.

Though I didn't believe it for a moment
I knew it was him by the set
of his shoulders and head, that physique
and the all but forgotten lift
of my heart at the sight of him.

For an instant he was alive
or I had died, though I knew
neither could be true and pressed on

to the post office past my friend
with the present that needed weighing,
more or less knowing nothing
was impossible, even heaven.

Nightingales

Who wouldn't feel a bit low
biking back into town again
from another vain after supper
ride round our nightingale woods
where they're two or three weeks overdue,
and though it's worrying what we've done,
it's a warm still evening – perfect
for hearing them sing – and being
in no hurry to go in
I pedal on past my turning
to check if it's true our local
The Volunteer, shut up for years,
against the odds has reopened,
and yes, it's alive, lights, music
and inside this Saturday night
as I swing round the corner
a good crowd of mostly young men
in both bars with more arriving
down the side street, one of whom
in reply to my *Evening* calls out –
Take your beret off, you cunt.

Between Two Lit Rooms

After work, for once, to walk home
not to drive, foot hinged to the clutch,
through town, but to walk on your own
out into the open dark,
the Plough, the Pole Star, Orion
distancing you from your day.
Then down the ringing wrought-iron
spiral staircase to the softer
asphalt of the all but empty
car park. One January night.
Such space around you, such plenty:
a good fifteen minutes walking
between two lit rooms, the split halves
of your life, the future, the past.
But for now a skive down this path,
the ridge of the fence furred with frost.

Between Ourselves

Vertical now more
often this week, you reach

up for a hand, a hooked
finger or two's enough

to hold on to to keep
your balance, your feet

staggering us from room to room,
across gravel and the rough

grass with its tufts and dips
I never minded before

this having to get a grip
round your whole hand

or wrist in case you trip,
which you must dislike –

you try shaking me off.
Not that I'll let you

go yet or let go myself
of this half hour of us

together gadding about
in step more or less,

my stoop and the inches
the nurse at the doctors'

insists that I've shrunk
advantageous for once,

bringing us close.
Though you won't remember

this morning I'm writing
it down by hand, a fond

old man, leaving these words
behind, typed up, online,

hoping they may come in
some day and steady you

now you're on your own.

The Last Swim

September, October ... one thing
you don't know at the time is when
you've had your last swim: the weather
may hold, may keep nudging you in.

Only afterwards, sometimes days on,
it dawns on you that you've done:
just the thought of undressing outdoors,
exposing bare skin, makes you wince.

And that's best, to have gone on swimming
easily to the end: your crawl
full of itself, and the future
no further than your folded towel.

One Job of Mine

this time of year's the woodburner.
It's my spit spat on newspaper
unsmokes the glass, my headstrong axe
that splits the logs approximately
where I want. I lay the fire
(the kindling's Kay, she brings some home
from all our walks) and though we never
keep it in overnight, the room's
still warm when I come in to start
again. I nurse the ashpan through
the house and out. Today grey flakes
of deadpan ash go whirling off.

Taken from the *Collected Poems*, November 2025
https://poetrybusiness.co.uk/product/michael-laskey-collected-poems/

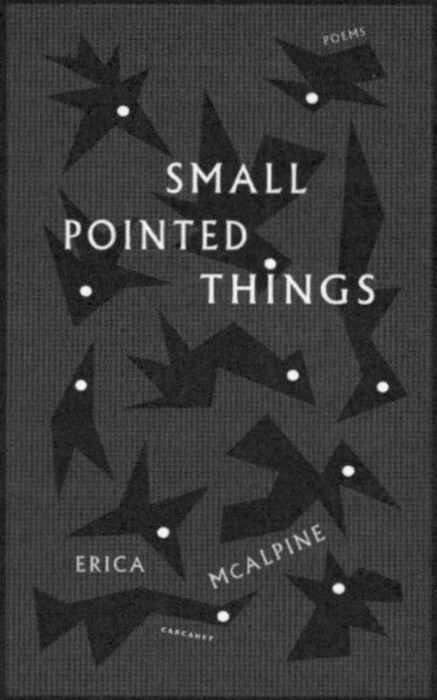

New Poets Prize

The following poems are by our two Winners for 2024/25, chosen by Holly Hopkins.

WINNER OF THE 2024 NEW POETS PRIZE

notes on burials
JAYANT KASHYAP

Pamphlet | 9781914914959 | £6
eBook | 9781914914966 | £4.50

June 2025

An archaeological dig, a visit to an imagined London, puppies that come back from the dead. In *Notes on Burials* Jayant Kashyap makes a series of journeys: real, mythological and etymological as he navigates what is lost and what is buried. Kashyap's poems of love and remembrance reach out to collective losses, human and environmental, in a series of disappearing acts and excavations that take us from broken childhood patio to a snowboarder in an avalanche.

Jayant Kashyap is an Indian poet and author of two previous pamphlets, *Unaccomplished Cities* (Ghost City Press, 2020) and *Survival* (Clare Songbirds, 2019), and a zine, *Water* (Skear Zines, 2021). Kashyap won the Young Poets Competition at the Wells Festival of Literature in 2021, and was awarded a Toto Award for Creative Writing in 2025.

In these tender poems, definitions, etymologies and repetitions perform a kind of excavation, digging to the root-places but also layering back up, hand over hand, word over word, to build a language of grief that feels fractured and true.
— Miriam Nash

Jayant Kashyap's Notes on Burials *asks the reader to consider different types of burials and retrievals, including personal and etymological burials, in cool, reflective poems.*
— Holly Hopkins

JAYANT KASHYAP

Notes on Burials

bury (v.): to put or hide underground; to cover completely;

from *borrow*, *borough*, or from *Burg* (German), which is
'to fortify'

as in to protect; as in
to provide – with possessions: food, pots

and pans, things to wear and even a toothbrush and a comb
– this physical manifestation of life

when the soul travels to the gods

*

it is said a burial is holding on to the dead
so the body – this cold

soil; cloth – is taken in a ship
along water, as in water between earth and heaven, or hell;

water, as in Styx, or Vaitarani –

*

and some burn their dead before

because fire purifies, because souls cling

to the material, this physical

manifestation; but 'oh to be free' of oneself,
'with nothing left to remember'

*

and I'm putting some earth on the grave of a friend's friend
to say this is what we give you for rest

that while the wait is long – and it always is – when god
is here he will know you were loved

– we'll have found ways to tell him

this; and that you never knew death

On the finding of a body, said to be the result of a drug overdose
<small>23 Feb, 2023; Prayagraj, India</small>

Mother, our home is burning. Aren't we all
made out of funeral pyres?

The fact that we want
to know nothing perhaps does it.

Yesterday, they found a body

in the university campus:
he was young – whoever that boy was;

his mouth had frothed out like soap-
water. Somewhere some-

thing had burnt and he had embraced it.

It won't make news
because events like this scar names.

They say he was of some religion –
practising – and in bad company. A grave

has been dug.
Another body will occupy the earth's drying

dying belly.
– And soon, there will be people

throwing words at each-other
where the body was found.

WINNER OF THE 2024 NEW POETS PRIZE

lobe
CIA MANGAT

Pamphlet | 9781914914973 | £6
eBook | 9781914914980 | £4.50

June 2025

A gold bangle, a barbershop and Diana Princess of Wales in an Indian wedding video. In Lobe, Cia Mangat navigates what we inherit and what we leave behind in a book which plays with private and public mythologies. These poems create a world of love and surveillance, where Diana's revenge dress prepares for the paparazzi and aunties gossip in the threading parlor. Bodies are pierced and cut from magazines while the wedding halls beckon. Lobe is a book of resistance and reimagining, where Di escapes her buttercream wedding, a woman shaves her head and 'george michael will sing every song you have ever wanted   to you /directly   accompanied by hundreds of thousands of people you love'.

Cia Mangat is a poet from London. Her work has been published in fourteen poems, *gal-dem*, *Propel*, and *bath magg*, and has been broadcast by the BBC. She founded and edited *Zindabad*, a zine for people in diasporas worldwide, and facilitates writing and zine-making workshops.

Lobe! *I love it. What a gorgeous debut. Playful, original, funny and beautiful all at once, these poems sing with the small intimacies of women's lives and of family dynamics as well as navigating the journey to living in your body and your life on your own terms. Sublime.*
  – Cecilia Knapp

Punk, princess, scissor-sharp, jewellike, each poem is a riot, is a revelation. This is the collection every (immigrant) mother, auntie, and all of her nieces, some nephews, and closest confidants have been waiting to gossip about. A thrilling new voice in poetry!
  – Rachel Long

CIA MANGAT

inventory of aunties

ageing aunty with milky eyes that can barely make out
the lights in the gurdwara hall; aunty with laugh that peels
down southall broadway like cheap rhinestones off a suit;
new aunty so richly perfumed with incense that her nieces
shrink in horror; aunty with swollen wrists, bangles biting
into the flesh; aunties chewing; aunties chopping onions;
twenty or thirty aunties who swap salwars in the colours
of parakeets & perch at the back of the langar hall, watching;
twenty more with swollen arteries & beige bra straps, laser
hair removal leaflets in their purses; aunties chopping garlic;
aunty whose fingers begin with gold bands folded into flesh
& end with tips rooted in her daughters' oiled scalps; aunty
always clamouring to name the newest baby; aunties chopping
ginger; aunty licking haldi off her finger; aunties on whatsapp;
aunty wearing your eyes; aunty wearing your mouth; aunty
wearing your nose; aunty whose face you don't even know
reaching to unclasp her chain & press it into your palms

sometimes I wonder if my ma is right & I do actually fancy boys

           but then again it is only ever the backs of their heads
    boys bending over to tie their shoelaces or pray
                      boys disappearing
down escalators
           never the blueness of their gazes   or   their mouths
maybe I fancy boys less than I do the steadiness of their barbers' hands
        when I shaved my head   I did it without a mirror & my hands shook
              so I started going to boys' barbers instead
the first asked where the darkness in my hair is from & insists we are brothers
                gives me the same haircut as him
   & I don't fancy this man
but in the wetness of the mirror   I fancy myself more than ever

my new barber laughs & laughs at the idea of me being mistaken for an italian
as he presses the clippers to my neck   he asks me what I want   & gives it to me once a month
   last time we saw each other   he used a pair of scissors to neaten the sides of my head
   & while he sliced the black   he said aloud that I must have been beautiful
when my hair was long   so thick it could trap sunlight & metabolise it into darkness
           sometimes before I leave the house my ma stops me in the kitchen
only for a minute dots kajal behind one of my ears against nazar
        & tucks the blemish   smudged secret
when I get haircuts from my barber   I am covered   with small black lines
  for the rest of the day like miniature ants swarming a fruit

        sometimes he leaves a smudge of it on my neck & I swear

      boys look straight through me

New Poets Prize

The following poems are by our two Runner up Poets for 2024/25, chosen by Holly Hopkins.

ZELDA CAHILL-PATTEN

Zelda Cahill-Patten lives and works in London. Her poems have been published in Magma, Sheila-Na-Gig and Ink Sweat & Tears. She has been awarded the Lord Alfred Douglas Memorial Prize (University of Oxford, for poetry in strict rhyming metre) and the Gertrude Hartley Poetry Prize (Balliol College). Her nonfiction writing on medieval tomb sculpture was awarded the Henry Moore Dissertation Prize in 2024.

CHARLIE JOLLEY

Charlie Jolley is a young poet and music journalist from Sheffield. She was a winner of the Foyle Young Poets of the Year Award in both 2023 and 2024, and commended in the Tower Poetry Competition 2025. She has performed at festivals such as Off The Shelf and the Making Waves Arts Festival, and has been published by The Poetry Society, Verve Poetry Press, and EDGE Magazine. She is an alumnus of Sheffield Young Writers and a member of Hive Poetry Collective.

NEW POETS LIST

ZELDA CAHILL-PATTEN

Pelias

> '*Why do you hesitate, so timidly?*' she said. '*Un-sheath your blades, and let out the old blood, so that I can fill the empty veins with new!*'
> – Ovid, Metamorphoses

We wash our hands, so sallow, lingering, slight.
The peeler sings; the carrot, neatly flayed,
is bright, its orange flush-like beneath greyed,
dull, dusky skin; its rawness never quite
expected. Now the coughs of pillared steam
rise from the kettle, and we lift the top
from yet another pan. And now we lop
the hair off from a leek and take some cream,
and add it. Oh, the metal-bellied pot
might hiss, the tea might scald, the soup might not
be salted to his liking, mummified,
dank, pallid, sour. Still, the beef is fried,
and sweet. We wonder, is this all he needs?
He looks so discontented as he feeds.

Redwood After Wildfire

A snowfall of dark ash
has muffled this forest.

Fire scars hold the memory:
scent of boiled sap
on hot winds,

trees glittering
with bright autumnal tongues —
ember-rich, then black.

In the hush the redwood
releases her cones, perfect
as earth-coloured eggs.

From this charcoal waste
her shoots will rise:

green flames, flickering
for the sun.

CHARLIE JOLLEY

Sid Vicious Walks Alone on Brooklyn Bridge, 1978

He's decided to pack it all in. Done with the punk-
professed pub-goers, the women drenched in steel,
songs unspooling like decades, he no longer wants

to buckle under the brick-swinging emptiness of fame,
or the gothic bones of his childhood, his blunt-needled
body softly slipping into sagging shirts as if dressing

a wound. He wants to do things His Way, have kids,
settle down, wear brailled fishing jumpers for parents'
evenings, beige ties for best. He wants Nancy and him

to join couples' yoga, drain pale pints on Friday nights
and tune into Corrie's Christmas spesh. He's swapping
his bass for a buggy, his Special Brew for a brew.

Mr Vicious wants to listen to Radio 4 on family holidays
while passing round buttery mints, as they trundle
along a grey vein of motorway. Sid walks alone

on Brooklyn Bridge, hair dark and arrowed, sneakers
faded as newsprint. He keys his padlocked chain until
it unclamps, and tosses it into the lip of a wave.

Sid knows deep down – you can't cling to the past
like a bad dream, living as a ghost in a life you once
knew, where every tomorrow is just one long today.

Tomorrowland

In the future, everything will be perfect again.
There'll be no more wars, no paint-splatter
gunfire or planes crashing from the skies
like dead whales. The monarchy will have vanished,
Kings and Queens no longer penned in their prisons
like chess pieces, while the world outside slowly
burns. There'll be no wageless nurses weeping
through too-short sandwich breaks, no parentless kids
or childless mothers, social media swipes, Instagram
likes, pimpled teenagers punishing their suffocating skin.
No sleeping on the streets or struggling to eat, no
long walks home clutching keys like a dagger,
waiting for catcallers and bellyfulls of broken laughter.
In the future, humans won't exist. Just the space
they leave behind, like an empty cardboard box.
That will be all that remains. That, and the sequined sky.
The miles and miles of red-scorched earth.

Two new books on the life and work of revered Jewish-Soviet Poet Semyon Izrailevich Lipkin from Hendon Press

Until recently, Semyon Izrailevich Lipkin (1911–2003) was best known in the West for his role in preserving the manuscript of Vasily Grossman's *Life and Fate* from the KGB. These volumes, translated by award-winning poet Yvonne Green, comprise *Testimony*, a memoir of Lipkin's friendships with Anna Akhmatova, Martina Tsvetaeva and Grossman himself and *A Close Reading*, translations of 53 of Lipkin's own, wonderful poems chosen by Alexander Solzhenitsyn.

Both books are available priced £14.99 direct from the Poetry Business website at https://poetrybusiness.co.uk/ or from Amazon.

The witty, wise and acerbic voice of Semyon Lipkin, a poetic scourge of Soviet autocracy and cruelty, comes fully to life in this volume. Hendon Press, Yvonne Green and Sergei Makarov are to be congratulated for this precious poetic gift to the English-language reader.

– Thomas de Waal, author of *The Caucasus: An Introduction* and translator of Osip Mandelstam's *Tristia*

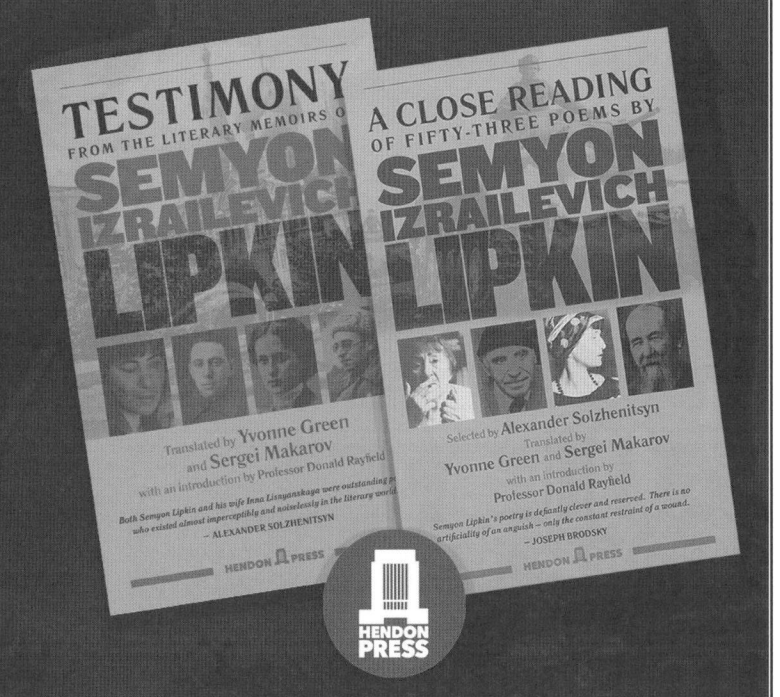

Longbarrow Press

Visionary, urgent … truly extraordinary blendings of environmental and social history. It swept me along. Mark Wormald

This spirited, astonishing, bewildering collection is one of the best long poems I have read. Adam Piette

Eely is a symphony in four movements. This book-length poem by **Steve Ely** explores themes of fenland, power, conflict and biodiversity, and the lifecycle, ecology, epic migration, conservation status and enigma of the European eel.

Eely is available now in hardback from **Longbarrow Press.**

www.longbarrowpress.com

Storegga

Daybreak in the wreck of Dogger. Gulls drifting
over the slowly rising sea. Seals hauled out
on sandbanks, bleached ribs of stranded whales.
Dunlin and knot, swarming the mudflats,
armies of silt-spearing godwit and whaup.
Butterbumps booming from brackish phragmites,
gorged on the bootlace bounty. Harriers
quartering over. Campfire wisp from the holme's relief
in the pearl of the roseate dawn; boat slides
from creek into tidal waters, trailing
its fuchsia ripple. Paddles out under chatter
of pinking terns, the flushed conflagrations
of billionfold gyring flamingos.

Steve Ely

THE 2024 INTERNATIONAL BOOK & PAMPHLET *Competition*

Winner of the 2024 International Book & Pamphlet Competition, selected by Jane Clarke

BOY, MOTHER

Caroline Bracken

Pamphlet | 9781914914911 | £6.00
eBook | 9781914914928 | £4.50
6 March 2025

Caroline Bracken's poems have been published in *The North*, *Poetry Wales*, *Poetry News*, *Gutter*, *New England Review*, the *Irish Times*, the *Honest Ulsterman*, *Belfield Literary Review*, *Poetry Jukebox* and elsewhere. She won the 2023 Renard Press Kinship Poetry Competition and has been a finalist in the Manchester Poetry Prize, Aesthetica Creative Writing Award, Tennessee Williams & New Orleans Festival Poetry Contest and Alpine Fellowship Poetry Prize.

Boy/Mother is a deeply moving exploration of a mother's relationship with her son who has a long-term mental illness. In innovative forms the poems evoke the day-to-day depredations of illness, psychiatric treatment and societal attitudes and yet the thread that runs through the collection is love.

— Jane Clarke

CAROLINE BRACKEN

Black Coat

I could say that the words gone missing are far too close to *gone fishing* and the term *misper* as shorthand for *missing person* makes me throw up. What I will say is that when he disappeared the thought crossed my mind that if the worst happened, my black coat had seen better days, was certainly unfit for a son's funeral and replacing it right then was out of the question in case I'd be tempting fate and if the worst actually happened it would not be the time to go shopping so the coat would have to do and it really didn't matter one way or the other so why was I even worried about it? Then he was found and I forgot all about the black coat because I didn't need it and have not needed it since and maybe will never need it and please God he will be the one in need of a black coat for my final disappearance and I will make sure he has one ready so he won't have to think about it and a black coat will be the last thing on his mind and he can say something poetic to describe my disappearance and he can talk about the day we went shopping for his black coat and it won't be morbid at all, it might even be amusing and it will be a fine black coat with plenty of wear in it.

The Blues

The men in white coats don't wear white coats any more
    they wear grey sports jackets and open-necked shirts
        expensive ones
            in unthreatening colours
                duck-egg blue   champagne pink   cornsilk yellow

Sometimes the men not in white coats are women
    who wear dresses covered in fleur-de-lis patterns
        or tea-green tops
            with navy culottes
                and genuine leather tan Chelsea ankle boots

Their nails are French-polished and their hair is bobbed
    neither short nor long but cut just below the chin
        sprayed in position
            no ribbons   no scrunchies
                trimmed every six weeks   tell-tale roots covered

None of the men or women wear jewellery except for a wedding band
    unlike their clients who wear rings on all fingers including thumbs
        they have ear   nose   tongue
            and belly-button piercings
                tens of chains around their throats and wrists

All must be relinquished on admittance   a single sleeper earring
    could be fatal   strings are cut from tracksuit bottoms
        laces ripped from Docs
            belts unleashed from jeans
                so the incompetent become experts in knot-tying
And running barefoot.

Fabric
after Anne Carson

'His mother saw it mothers are like that'—
they work with invisible thread
sewing cloth or lace so that mendings
blend into the weave
long after danger has passed
you refuse red meat
dine only on white:
bread, pasta, vanilla ice-cream
your brother's head xylophoning the bannisters
the ambulance
and the black maria
waiting
Let me fetch my needle
slip stitch your thoughts
hold them in place
with this unbreakable thread
almost good as new

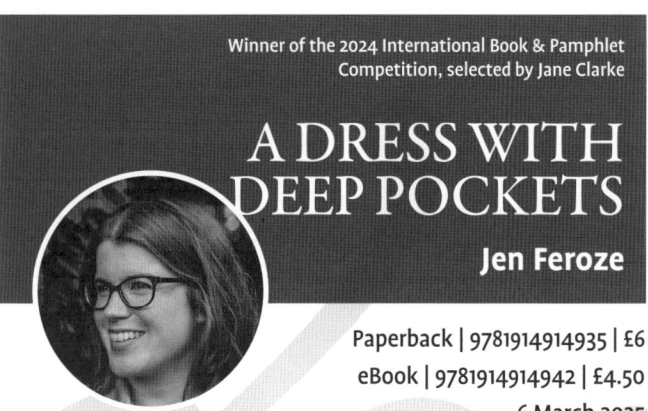

Winner of the 2024 International Book & Pamphlet Competition, selected by Jane Clarke

A DRESS WITH DEEP POCKETS

Jen Feroze

Paperback | 9781914914935 | £6
eBook | 9781914914942 | £4.50
6 March 2025

Jen Feroze lives by the sea in Essex. A former Foyle Young Poet, her work has appeared in publications including *Poetry Wales, Under The Radar, Magma, The Interpreter's House, And Other Poems, Berlin Lit* and *Butcher's Dog*. She placed second in the 2022/2023 Magma Editors' Prize and was highly commended in the 2021 Spelt competition. Jen has edited anthologies for Black Bough Poetry and The Mum Poem Press, and her debut pamphlet *Tiny Bright Thorns* was published by Nine Pens in 2024.

A lightness of touch combined with wit and insight distinguishes A Dress with Deep Pockets. *The collection addresses themes of loss and change through memories of people and place and above all friendship. Here are poems that celebrate, offer solace and resonate far beyond the page.*
— Jane Clarke

JEN FEROZE

I invite my grown-up daughter round for dinner

Which is odd, because she's seven
and building something complicated out of Lego
while the oven chips cook.
It's late summer, and in my head

I'm making her a salad: Prosciutto
and fresh peaches. A nice bottle of French wine.
I find I've tidied up
as if she were a minor royal and not the girl

who once trailed coco pops up the stairs.
I must remember to ask her how work is going,
whether she feels fulfilled. Whether she still laughs
like a five-star hotel sink draining.
Whether they make her laugh, slinging their arm
around her shoulders with ease. Does she still bounce
on the balls of her feet when waiting to speak?
Do blossom trees still make her sad?
The doorbell rings.
The oven timer rings.
She'll be taller. I won't be.
That's all I really know.

The four of us in August

This is friendship like a jersey dress.
Comfortable and smart
with deep pockets.

The children are finally sleeping, sprawled
long-limbed and ringletted
across the big bed. Outside,
the four of us scrape garden chairs closer
to the fire pit, slosh more of the good wine
into our glasses. Owls
glimmer in the trees, the moors
are within touching distance.

We're talking careers, future shaping;
mapping our collective middle age –
the same slightly outraged expression
mirrored on each of our faces.
We're mopping the last of the oil from our plates
with crusts of bread. Now the fire is like water,
lapping against the memory of wood.

We watch the sparks climb
feeling special and ancient as stars.
Later, in bed, my skin
smells pleasingly of smoke.

Grief: A Primer

It wasn't Beth March.
It was a bat named, I believe,
Vesper, who was deeply in love
with a squirrel princess.

He was a sparky bat.
A wry, gentlemanly bat,
and me and Em had serious crushes
on him. We finished that mad old
wedge of a book at the same time,
sitting in the bottom of her wardrobe
with a blanket over our knees.

Knowing what was coming
and sobbing our preteen hearts out.
Amazed that words on a page
could do that. The audacity.
He was perfect for us.
Perfect.

Except, you know,
he was a fictional bat.
And now he was dead.

THE 2024 INTERNATIONAL BOOK & PAMPHLET *Competition*

The following poems are by our two Runners Up and three Commended Poets for 2024/25, chosen by Jane Clarke.

RUNNERS UP

Dale Booton

Dale Booton (he/him) is a queer poet from Birmingham. His poetry is published by *The North* and *Magma*, and anthologised by Broken Sleep Books, Verve, Muswell Press, and Pan Macmillan. He has two pamphlets out: *Walking Contagions* (Polari Press) and *On This Stretch of Queerland* (Fourteen Poems).

Kate Rutter

is an actor and poet. Her recent credits include Better for BBC, The Long Shadow for ITV and Truelove for Channel 4. Films she's appeared in have won The Palme D'or, an Oscar and been nominated for BAFTAs. Her poems have been published in *The Rialto*, *The North*, *Strix*, *Magma* and several anthologies. She has been runner up in The Bridport Prize and in The Poetry Business, Mslexia (Bloodaxe) and Magma pamphlet competitions.

COMMENDED

James Appleby

is the author of the upcoming pamphlet *Spurious Language*. He lives in Edinburgh and is the editor of Interpret, Scotland's new magazine of international writing.
www.jamesapplebywriting.co.uk /
www.interpretmagazine.com

Ger Duffy

lives in Co. Waterford, Ireland. Her poetry and fiction has been published by Slow Dancer Press, The Women's Press, The Viking Press and Sheba Press. She holds a PG DIP in Creative Writing from Goldsmiths College, an MA in Screenwriting from University of Westminster, London.

Derval Tubridy

is an Irish poet whose work responds to the intimate traces that bind and blind. Born in Bandon, Co. Cork, she is now based in Dublin. Professor Emerita of Goldsmiths, London, she is the author of Thomas Kinsella: The Peppercanister Poems (UCD Press, 2001) and Samuel Beckett and the Language of Subjectivity (Cambridge UP, 2018).

DALE BOOTON

Mocks

they scarper like sheep having heard the gnawing bark
of a dog   or quick-drop like startled goats
at the sight of my sus shadow around corridor corners
draw coat hoods up   faceplant blazered-arms   wear planners
as masks   but the next day they are quick to ask
whether they've been marked   all 26 of them with
4 papers a body   demand answers to their performance
*how did I do on the Shakespeare sir   did you read what I wrote about
masculinity and how Lady Macbeth proper rips Macbeth
to shreds   was my article good sir   was it Edwardian era
or Jacobean*   it was Victorian and from what I've skimmed
very few have answered the poetry   and have misread the lines
for a language paper   so little written means fewer marks probably
they say *don't worry sir   we'll try harder for the real ones*

Beyond

*yeah but sir if ya don't believe in the afterlife
then why'd ya say bloody hell*   the logic is irrefutable
they can tell from my face that I have nothing to say
quickly move on   *what do ya think
happens when ya die then*   we've been told
not to surpass our wandering
beyond those grassy realms of educational fact
into selfish belief   but I do
offer my opinion   door open   palm flat
*but that isn't a happy end is it like   don't ya believe
in anything*   I tell them *I believe in you lot
in my family   my friends*   a pink mist
of sentiment settles over a classroom for a second
then the erasing power of laughter   *like you've got friends*

POETRY BOOK SOCIETY RECOMMENDATION

VERSUS VERSUS

100 POEMS BY DEAF, DISABLED & NEURODIVERGENT POETS

Edited by Rachael Boast

available now from
BLOODAXE BOOKS

www.bloodaxebooks.com

KATE RUTTER

Through All This

I've loved sleeplessness: sunrise
creeping over a Sheffield hill.

I've loved your screen face, far away
and buffering but still yours.

I've loved the shock of your hair
clipped to the length of a skull cap.

I loved that when I picked up it was you
and though you chided yourself

for crying in a car park,
I loved that you felt you could.

I've loved the book about molluscs
my sister and brother-in-law sent

and the astonished snails I carried
to higher ground after reading it.

I've loved the cheerful deliveries,
the substitutions I always accept.

I've loved Maureen next door being
wheeled out to smoke her way through it.

I've loved the rain, the cleansing rain,
the sheer flattening weight of it

and the mud that almost stole my boot
in Monsal Dale and the bilberries

foraged that day that would do us good,
their juice purple as renewed blood.

Cable Car

We're in a side street eating fish kebabs
giant prawns   sea bream   squid on a stick
the moon's outshone by halogen lights
strung across the square   no stars
you say tomorrow we'll climb to Telemos
for the view   I know there's no such place
you only dreamt it   but we may take
a cable car to the top of somewhere
me with eyes tight shut all the way.

JAMES APPLEBY

Whale at distance

It is lost here; dying. It has strung the rope
of a buoy about the base of its fluke, or, or,
we watchers air our theories during dives,
brained by a motorboat. It is sick.
We are anchored one side of the firth,
mountains the other, and in the shipping lane,
under the eastbound freight is the great whale.
Juvenile, someone said, and now we all agree,
only a juvenile would dare. A whale at distance,
you must understand, is mostly the idea of a whale,
and conversations of this kind must go on,
because there is no leaping between ships,
no eye to meet, no barnacled face, only
thrills of fin among imposter waves
or the briefest fart of blowhole – enough
to drag us followers from our mornings
every morning, and under the freight of coal
or microwaves or papaya, touch something vast,
lungfelt, living, sick. Two weeks in view of the city
the whale ate and surfaced, came no closer
than the shallow centre of the shipping lane,
refused all lenses, would not be narrated,
then in new strength chased the cargo ships
into the broad sea, our juvenile. Like parents,
sharers in something, we are sitting in our homes,
like the collected bystanders to a miracle,
each subtly bettered and unbalanced.

Given a night of ice

Given a night, ice names everything,
pays its attention to each stone,
needle frost like concentrated thought
up from the moss to finger-height,
evacuates snails, January frog
rimed asleep under a stone,
river in fresh linen, frost willows
trailing their long hair languid in ice,
mapping the waterpath, instructing current,
helmets of ice on the stones at fast water,
fast under, over fast, hovering ice,
city deer gathering under the bridge,
us in our unfit boots unsteady
as a new love, taking new care
of things we have done so often,
and so
    when I hear that ice is cruel

GER DUFFY

Testimony of Soap

i.m. the women and children held in Mother & Baby Homes, 1922- 1998 whose testimonies have been erased by the Irish State.

"And darkness and worms shall be their dwelling place"
(after Ishion Hutchinson)

ashamed soap   baby soap   birth soap blood soap
boarded out soap   buried soap   childrens' allowance soap
churched soap   confined soap   decades of the rosary soap
dehydration soap   destitute soap   discarded baby soap
fallen women soap   glaxo smith klein soap
horrified soap   human remains soap   illegitimate soap
inferior sub species soap   jaundiced soap   keep going soap
lack of consent soap   laundry soap   lice soap   locked up soap
malnutrition soap   marmarus soap   mass grave soap
mastitis soap   naked soap   order of the bons secours soap
panic soap   penitent soap   pregnant soap   premature soap
punishment soap   rape soap   rat soap   remembrance soap
scrubbed soap   sexual abuse soap   signed away soap
silenced soap   stitched soap   sewerage soap   sin soap
shocked soap   skeletal soap   slave soap   sold soap
trafficked soap   unmarked grave soap   unmarried soap
unpaid soap   unwashed soap vanished soap   witness soap

Hotpants

My tender bud breasts, downy fur under my armpits
and down below, surprised me daily. Grown men spoke
to my breasts when I served them in my father's shop.
My older sister bought me a skinny tight tee-shirt
with lurid yellow hotpants. My ponytail became a low
side tail, I stole my sister's frosted blue eyeshadow
and pink wet look lipstick. Boys at the tennis club,
hid behind hedges to watch porn magazines, while
us girls sat on benches and waited. We waited
until they were ready, when we all squashed
into a viewing box to play the game. The game
involved giving each other marks out of ten for sex
appeal. I usually got a six or seven, my hot pants
elevated me to a nine. One girl was told she had no score
as her face did not compute, the boys thought this hilarious.
She often stayed after we left. She would emerge after
we drank our cokes, red faced, muzzled haired, eyes averted.

DERVAL TUBRIDY

Late

I'm late again. The brother doesn't want
to go to school. The elder sister teases,
toys with his frustrations until tears.

Then she's out the door, green flash
of gaberdine whips up to the bus stop:
darts across the dual carriageway,
scrambles up to the top deck.

I join her the next year. Two hands on the banister
as the bus swings and sways. A pocket full
of crumpled tickets (which one for the inspector?)
Everyone is smoking.

My coat is soaked. I sneak it into the boiler room.
On the way home Mam is cross about the nuns,
the way they keep half nuns, ones who aren't full
nuns, who launder and clean (I like our nuns).

She moves him to another school.
But still he's acting up.

Only later, much later, reading those reports,
watching the halting witness on the television,
      I reach for the phone.

Window

Mock orange blossoms whiten against a grey
concrete outhouse. Brambles tap against
its tin roof, corrugated against rain.

Ash sways behind, grown strong from the sapling I planted
in a cracked cinderblock lying against the skeleton
of a wheelbarrow, on the reflex angle between two fields.

A box hedge, large and obstreperous, against its better nature.
Honeysuckle sweetens against a rough low wall,
and loganberry confuses everything by not being sure.

I lie in the light of morning on a green wrought iron bed,
bought to guard against Spanish flu. Brass finials glint
against a white distemper wall. My breath against you.

'Black Tie at the Mansion House'

A Foreign Country
Nigel Pantling
Paperback | 978-1-914914-45-4 | £10.99
eBook | 978-1-914914-46-1s | £6.99
April 2025

In *A Foreign Country,* Nigel Pantling takes us to some strange places – the exotic, the imaginary and the rediscovered past – and for each he serves up a heady local brew, equal parts memory, invention, wit and menace. Here, North Korean tourists rub shoulders with Syrian adventurers, the newly dead with a City lothario, Popeye and Olive Oyl with Cold War warriors. Surprising and unsettling by turns, these poems are a whistle-stop journey through different times, countries and customs, enriched by deep personal experience.

Praise for Nigel Pantling's previous collections:

Nigel Pantling's poems lift the lid on worlds closed to most of us. In language that is straightforward and precise, subtly ironic, he lets facts tell their own, often shocking, story.
  – Carole Satyamurti

Timely, satirical and razor-sharp poems.
  – Michael Symmons Roberts

Focusing on a wide range of entirely convincing characters and situations, his entertaining short story poems have the accumulated power of a long and absorbing novel.
  – Michael Laske

Nigel Pantling's pamphlets *Belfast Finds Log* (Shoestring Press, 2014) and *Hip Hind Hook* (Smith|Doorstop, 2018) relate the danger and human frailty he saw during Northern Ireland's Troubles and the Cold War. His full collections *Kingdom Power Glory* and *It's Not Personal* (Smith|Doorstop, 2016 and 2020) lift the lid on the secrets of Whitehall and the City, and on the eccentricities of work and the unpredictability of family, love and death.

NIGEL PANTLING

Pit Stop

Tired tourists, just debussed
at a truck-stop with no fuel
on a road that surely must
one day run on down to Seoul,

write 'Great Leader' in the dust,
waiting for their tea to cool
wonder if the taste of rust
is another *Juche* rule,

leave their bread – it's mostly crust –
(longing for the guide to call)
smile and shake their heads non-plussed
at the drabness of it all,

hope that somewhere out the back
kids are drinking, playing pool,
laughing at the clack and smack
of coloured ball on coloured ball.

A String of Pearls
from 30 pages of Ripley's Believe it or Not.

Bagpipes were often played in Ancient Rome
Caligula made his favourite horse a consul
Cavalry captured the Danish fleet by crossing the frozen sea
Madame de la Bresse left her fortune to clothe snowmen
Monsieur Wzs is a native of the village of Ws
Z. Z. Zizz is an engineer on the Northern Pacific Railroad
A Fortunat Mann lives in Indianapolis
I. Etta Hamburgher is buried in Madison Cemetery
Cheese can be sliced more thinly with a dull knife
A cucumber is a berry
A pound of raw cotton has been spun into a 2000 mile yarn
Aesop did not write Aesop's fables
The Chief Rabbi of Lithuania could recite 2500 books by heart
Cardinal Mezzofanti taught Cockney slang to Byron
Hell is in Norway
A Raaaaaal is a Danish eel
A clam has teeth
Santa Claus is the patron saint of thieves
The original 'chauffeurs' were robbers who burnt victims' feet
Miss Fanny Miles of Cincinnati had feet twenty-four inches long
All the males of the Colombière family have two left hands
'Ambidextrously' has over half the alphabet with no repetition
One half of one half divided by one half is one half
Einstein failed his college mathematics entrance exam
Tycho Brae had an artificial nose made of gold
A pound of gold weighs less than a pound of feathers
Eugene Myers slept in the same feather bed for sixty-six years
The soprano Carlo Farinelli could hold a note for six minutes
The violinist Racz Pali had 48 sons and each became a violinist
Nero did not play the fiddle, he played the bagpipes
Bagpipes were often played in Ancient Rome

Witness Statement

There was no panic.
All ranks were standing calmly well back from the gun platforms.
I smelt cordite and observed smoke around the damaged gun.

I located the senior officer present, and asked about casualties.
None of the gun detachment had been struck by metal debris.
I found this most surprising.

However, several had burns to exposed skin, all were deafened,
some were blinded, and the Number One was in such shock
he would not let go of the firing lanyard. I cut it from his grasp.

Close inspection confirmed the detonation of a shell in the breech.
The barrel had burst and peeled back like a banana:
several feet of rifled steel had vaporised.

The firing mechanism, projected back thirty feet,
had embedded in a tree trunk, taking with it on the way
the epaulette of the section commander.

That completes my report, Sir. In thirty years' service
I have seen nothing like this before.
It will take much technical investigation to uncover the cause.

Might I suggest that the Americans may be able to help.
My driver tells me that they lost several guns this way in Vietnam,
before they sold these on to us.

Looking for Tigers

After you died, I went to Nepal,
trekking in the Himalayas mainly,
but a few days in a tourist lodge
in the southern jungle, for tigers.

That first night, I was drinking gin,
waiting for a briefing from a guide,
when another guest asked me
"Are you Peter Pettinger?"

Of course, I had to disappoint him:
it seems P P was to join him there,
but was a no-show. Then I realised
this chap was Tony Hill. You know,

he was a subaltern in the Regiment,
years ago. You met him with me
several times, he came to the quarter,
probably had dinner with us there.

That set me thinking about chance:
the chance of bumping into Tony Hill,
of you inheriting a breast cancer gene,
of my seeing any tigers tomorrow.

An Inspector Calls

Yes, we're like any other hospitality business really.
The trick is to understand what our guests want,
to work out how long they expect to be here,
where they think they're going,
and then to keep them as happy as we can
for as long as they end up staying with us.

You're right, some guests don't enjoy their stay.
We've certainly had our difficult moments:
complaints about the food, the beds and so on.
But to be honest, when our guests are unhappy
it's generally because they're waiting to be told
when they'll move, and that's above my pay grade.

Actually, I'm proud of what we do: my staff are good,
and I think you'll agree our Trip Advisor rating
is quite excellent, given all the circumstances.
But don't take my word for it, find out for yourself,
feel free to walk around, talk to our current guests,
test the temperature.

Bosra

I'm up in the gods, not literally,
not with Bel or belligerent Baalshamin,
or Astarte or Atargatis, givers of fertility,
but theatrically, on the fifty-first tier
of a semicircle of black basalt blocks.

I'm sitting quite alone under the sun,
without benefit of the cloth shading
or misty spray of perfumed water
that cooled second century patrons,
so all I can manage is to stay still

and watch tourists from a waiting bus
walk purposefully on from the wings,
and imagining themselves unseen
hurtle through some Shaw or Wilde
or mangle "all the world's a stage",

and thanks to the acoustic skills of
Roman architects I hear each word.
Until the heat becomes too much
and I make my way down to give
my one-man rendering of Godot.

FEATURED TITLE

From Secrets Corner – Dean Parkin
£12 , The Garlic Press 2024,108pp

Dean Parkin was born in 1969 and grew up in Carlton Colville, a village near Lowestoft. He left school at sixteen to work at a printers and then a bookshop. From 1999 to 2015 he was part of The Poetry Trust team responsible for the annual international Aldeburgh Poetry Festival, ending up as Creative Director.

Dubbed 'Suffolk's unofficial Poet Laureate' by BBC Radio Suffolk, Dean has written poetry collections for adults and children – *The Swan Machine* (2014) and *The Bubble Wrap and Other Poems* (Smith/Doorstop 2017) – over twenty books of local history, and three one-man shows.

Dean Parkin is the Grayson Perry of poetry, celebrating ordinary people and finding the extraordinary in their lives with gentle yet acute humour, kindness and hope.
– Alicia Stubbersfield

DEAN PARKIN

Wallpaper

It's where you're from.
It's what you still see
even if it's not there.

It's not a carpark, it's your house.
The factory is a row of cottages.
The estate? The village beneath.

Like the wallpaper you remember
under the wallpaper in the front room
that's been knocked into one.

All that's left is in you
as flimsy as a memory.
Let's take a good look.

Norwich Keeper

I did tell him I played in goal
for the youth team, when
what I meant was, I went along
to a training session for schoolboys
when I was thirteen and got
a bit carried away. He knew
I was joking, didn't he
and months later I'd forgotten it
when he texted about a spare ticket
for Sunday's game at Carrow Road
and to meet him in the King's Arms
for a pre-match drink.
The bar packed with yellow and green
and there was Nick at the back,
thumbs up when he saw me
and bellowed – *Here he is!*
Here's the guy who used to play
for Norwich! All eyes on me
I nod and part the hushed crowd
as he waves me toward his table
and his mates, one of them
wants to buy me a drink, while another
gives up his seat because
it's not every day you meet someone
who's worn the No.1 jersey.

Removal Men Discuss My Boxes of Books

Shane is forty and says he's never
been into them,
Marvel comics yes.
Josh is thirty and still likes his
Harry Potters and that.
Drew is twenty and says he did read
a book for half an hour
once but wants to ask
Ever heard of a Kindle, Mate?

Other recent titles from The Garlic Press include

Elizabeth Cook, *The Sound of Rain*
Martin Hayden, *Green Burial*
Naomi Jaffa, *Driver*
John Lynch, *These Days*
Kath McKay, *Moving the Elephant*
Philip Rush, *Camera Obscura*
Jeni Smith, *Snickety Snack*
Mary Anne Woolf, *A Thing to be Shifted*

Go to https://www.michaellaskey.co.uk/shop

BLIND CRITICISM

In this feature we ask writers to respond to a poem without telling them the author. This time around **Alice Hiller**, **Rishi Dastidar** and **Ed Reiss** took the plunge. Author and poem details are given on the inside back cover.

The Bomber

The Windrush runs through field and village
before it becomes the Thames. Clear water
with waving weeds, minnows, sticklebacks;
and where it bends, boys, swimming, splashing,
floating on their backs, diving off the bank.
That's where I learnt to swim – a frantic
doggy-paddle that just kept me buoyant
and lifted my feet from the stones at the bottom.

That summer we lay on the bank and let the sun
dry us off. We heard, one glorious afternoon,
the grumbling engines of a plane, very low.
A Flying Fortress lumbered into view,
enormous with jagged holes in its fuselage,
staggering through the air, just above the willows.
I saw blue through gaps in the wings.

Amazed, frightened, we jumped to our feet and waved,
as if our frantic waving could keep him airborne.
And the man (we could see his face),
as he steered his wreck with hopes of
              reaching an airfield,
waved back at the naked boys on the Windrush bank.

ALICE HILLER

Poems find their ways towards meaning through their readers. There's risk in this process, but also trust, and generosity. For me, 'The Bomber' sets off in two opposite directions. Burnished by patriotism and derring do, the surface narrative gives a plain-spoken, boy's eye view of wartime summer afternoons by the Windrush in Gloucestershire. A second current flows through this, interrogating the ethics of conflict, and the exploitation of cultural framing as a form of sublimated propaganda.

Like Poussin's seemingly idyllic painting, 'Et in Arcadia Ego', 'The Bomber' is freighted with death. Rather than peasants clustered round a tomb in a pastoral landscape, we get "naked" boys spotting a wrecked plane above an iconic tributary of the Thames. Danger persists when we plunge into the first stanza's "Clear water/ with waving weeds, minnows, sticklebacks", and "boys, swimming, splashing,/ floating on their backs, diving off a bank". Fear motivates the speaker's "frantic/ doggy-paddle that just kept me buoyant", making "the stones at the bottom" feel like a layer of menace beneath the 1940s summer sunshine.

The "frantic" swimming also summons the shadows of children lost across wartime Europe and beyond, and in England's bombed cities, for whom escape was not an option. Sound reinforces this subtext. Concluding the first stanza, the three lines describing the swimming contain ten unvoiced plosive t's, which set off a chain of miniature, bomb-like detonations. The risk they engender is heightened by the additional sonic interplay between "buoyant", "stones" and "bottom",

> *Rather than peasants clustered round a tomb in a pastoral landscape, we get "naked" boys spotting a wrecked plane above an iconic tributary of the Thames.*

which threads back together elements the swimming aims to separate.

Contributing to this mood of gilded darkness, the poem's tone and setting are also infused with echoes of a series of 'classic' English texts, written at the height of the British Empire, variously celebrating riverside environments and child swimmers. From Charles Kingsley's *The Water Babies* of 1862-3, to Jerome K. Jerome's *Three Men in a Boat* of 1889, to Kenneth Grahame's *The Wind in the Willows* and Beatrix Potter's *The Tale of Mr Jeremy Fisher,* both from 1908, and Arthur Ransome's *Swallows and Amazons,* published from 1930, their narratives have frequently been conscripted to valorise Britishness, and British landscapes, as being of paramount value.

None of these literary celebrants of English waterways suggests that other social groups and nationalities are more acceptable to sacrifice. Yet prioritising one culture over another can – in times of war – become tacitly integrated into the argument for doing this, something the poem may be asking us to reflect on, through its subtle juxtapositions and layered narrative structure. Like an image on poster for wartime heroism and propaganda, the "Bomber" of the title is shown, wrecked by enemy fire, directly above the civilians whom its murderous missions were flown to protect.

Groups of people being of more, or less, worth were inherent to the Nazi 'rationale' for the Third Reich's programme of genocides. The Allied Commanders operated on less explicitly articulated assumptions when their bombers targeted German, then Japanese, civilian populations, and infrastructures, or declined to act against the concentration camps so as not to detract from the war effort. British Denial, economic policies and prioritised distribution similarly withheld timely food relief during the Bengal Famine of 1943, on the grounds that the deaths by starvation of Bengali land and waterway workers and their families were acceptable to safeguard food supplies to Allied troops.

Encouraging us to think about how, and why, things may be presented in certain ways, the diction of the second stanza turns to wartime clichés to characterise the "glorious afternoon" and "grumbling engines" which usher the "very low" "Flying Fortress" into the poem. Heavily armed, and able to travel high and fast, the Boeing B17 flew daytime raids over Germany, and was also legendary for being able to limp back to base after suffering enemy fire, as described here.

Potentially factually accurate, like the riverside setting, and the boys' vulnerable, unclothed bodies, the choice of plane detail would also seem to be more generally symbolic. B17s were responsible for 42.6%, or 640,000 tons, of the bombs dropped by the Allies over Nazi Germany between 1939-45, greater than any other single design of aircraft. "Enormous with jagged holes in its fuselage,/ staggering through the air, just above the willows", the wreck makes visible the death and destruction left in its wake, and suggests German bodies left injured or lifeless. Within the second stanza's soundscape, the long, mourning diphthongs of "low", "holes" and "willows", alongside the emptied out vowels of "view", "fuselage" and "blue", help render their absences palpable.

Half the length of the opening stanza, the final verse enacts truncation. Meanwhile, the description of the boys waving at the pilot, who may be facing his own death, recalls wartime photos of civilians saluting trains carrying troops to and from the coast, but also confronts us with the deaths they were dispatched to inflict on foreign soil. Sonically, the first stanza's explosive 't's return, in the "frightened" boys, and their "frantic" waving, explicitly linking the speaker's earlier panicked swimming with this death-in-life moment. A final twist comes when the pilot "waved back", acknowledging the humanity of the boys who saluted him, as explicitly as his bombs would have disregarded the humanity of those they murdered.

At each turn, the act of interpretation is left to the reader. We may be beguiled by the surface veneer of a remembered childhood afternoon, or move through this to experience the subtly coercive and insidious framing of 'patriotic' propaganda. Encouraging us to read 'The Bomber' as a coded and doubled narrative, is the *HMT Empire Windrush* being named for the poem's

A final twist comes when the pilot "waved back", acknowledging the humanity of the boys who saluted him ...

supposed river. Originally a 1930s German cruise ship called the *MV Monte Rosa*, the vessel was deployed by German forces until the Allies captured it in 1945, after which it became a troopship, and then finally carried 500 plus Caribbean men, women and children to Tilbury Docks in 1948, to help Britain in the project of postwar reconstruction.

RISHI DASTIDAR

In the manner of the object foregrounded in this poem, what follows will not be in a straight line, and have plenty of holes in it. Let's go …

1. For a poem that features an imminent crash landing of a plane, this is a weirdly quiet, too quiet poem. That first stanza, mostly scene setting, is watery softness and delicious sibilance. All those s-words, 'sticklebacks', 'swimming', 'splashing' – delightful. But also: it's misdirection on the part of the poet. Which is admirable.

2. The one exception to all the wafty cooing: 'frantic'. That's our tell that maybe something other than a idyllic childhood story is coming.

3. We are in England Profound, the England the world thinks is England: "The Windrush runs through field and village / before it becomes the Thames." The England that is taught that it has never been invaded, or at least not recently, and so that makes it special in some way, more than other countries.

4. The mood that's being evoked through the poem is the one we are familiar with from the Battle of Britain; we few and all that. All the men here, and the men in training – no women, obviously – are actual heroes, and carry the potential to be heroes, of a land where afternoons are generally more glorious than not.

5. And at the core of the mythos, at the core of the what makes the English hero more heroic than other nations' heroes is this living – well, near death – example of stoicism.

6. This is the distilled essence of the foundational myth of the postwar Britain that thinks it decolonised willingly, wasn't outgunned by an American empire, that chaps called Jacques and Helmut and Antonio aren't to be trusted. This is why we won. This is why we should still be winning.

7. The "Flying Fortress" is the grit, the fact that we have to go off, if we want to play detective here. And we do, so perhaps it's worth considering the following:

8. The Flying Fortress, the 'Bomber' of the title, is the Boeing B-17 Flying Fortress, as flown by the United States Army Air Forces (USAAF). They arrived in High Wycombe in 1942, to be part of the US's daylight strategic bombing campaign in Europe. This type of plane dropped more bombs than any other aircraft during World War II.

9. So if it was flying back over the Windrush, something has gone very wrong. As we can see.

10. Which means we come to the crux of the poem, the waving, which we assume on his part is not frantic, unlike that of the boys, where it is identified as such. This conveys much, not just about the pilot, about the whole self-image of the RAF, and by extension the way that we think about how the war was fought, and by further extension, Britain itself.

11. How true might it be though? How stoic might a man rapidly going down in a plane "staggering through the air" actually be? Here's a different perspective:

For a poem that features an imminent crash landing of a plane, this is a weirdly quiet, too quiet poem.

12. "At that moment, I felt a terrific explosion which knocked the control stick from my hand, and the whole machine quivered like a stricken animal. In a second, the cockpit was a mass of flames… I remember a moment of sharp agony, remember thinking 'So this is it!' and putting my hands to my eyes. Then I passed out."

13. This is from the 'Proem' of Richard Hillary's *The Last Enemy*. A memoir of his time fighting as a Spitfire pilot in the Battle of Britian, it was an instant bestseller in 1942, written after he had been shot down. Hillary died the year after, in a training accident.

14. (Incidentally, that title is biblical: "The last enemy that shall be destroyed is death", 1st Corinthians 15:26.)

15. Hillary was one of his generation's most dashing and beautiful men, an instant hero in a time that needed some, seeing as the 1930s produced none. Sebastian Faulks made him one of the subjects in *The Fatal Englishman*, a tripartite biography of promising lives cut short. In that, Faulks says that RAF pilots did not have to be reckless, patriots, thrill seekers. Rather, "they had to have, at heart, some indifference to dying. The public were encouraged by Churchill's speeches to believe this indifference was heroic; the pilots themselves did not see it as such … they cultivated understatement in private slang; they came close to callousness: they claimed to feel nothing."

16. Another resonance. Faulks again, on an early flight on the way to see action in the Battle: "Hillary wrote that they then flew down the valley where the children played and that with white boulders in the heather the children had spelled out the message 'Good Luck'. He later admitted that this was an invention: the children could not have known of the Air Ministry's orders."

17. At some deep level, we need our doomed pilots to become heroes, potential exemplars to children – become myths – and be stiff upper lip about it while doing so.

18. Also worth noting: of the three most consequential moments in the poem (the bomber being shot, the boys seeing the plane, and the crash landing) two of those happen off stage. What this means is that the language here doesn't have the noise, the crunch, the physicality you might otherwise expect.

19. Instead we are closer to a dream, or a very hazy memory. We're reading this poem for mood, not exactitude. Impressions of a moment, through simple language, simple images. The line that does that best for me: "I saw blue through gaps in the wings."

20. One other thing: Windrush. Let me merely observe that, the next time you hear anyone wondering why things can't be 'like they were before' or other such codes, remember, maybe even remind them: they came on a ship named after the most English river you can think of.

21. I'll leave you with a note that I think is mine, but could be Faulks' or even Hillary's (if so, forgive the unintended larceny): swagger and sang froid was actually fear disguised as indifference.

ED REISS

I recognise this as a poem by the late Gerard Benson, poet laureate of Bradford. So, I read it first as a memory of Gerard's boyhood in the south of England in the 1940s, although it may also contain something of folk memory. The ordinary language conveys a sense of the poet recalling an experience honestly, with no need for tricksiness.

We're reading this poem for mood, not exactitude. Impressions of a moment, through simple language, simple images.

When a poem has the art of hiding art, we may examine its art all the more closely, even if that entails stating the obvious. Here, the first sentence gives us a place: a river many of us won't know, connected to the Thames. The second sentence sketches what is happening in the place. The third sentence introduces the first person and tells us what the place means to that 'I'. The fourth sentence, starting the second stanza, homes in on the time ('That summer') while the fifth is more precise ('one glorious afternoon'). Here, ten lines in, halfway through the poem, begins the central incident, followed by the boys' response to the incident; and how the pilot responded to them. The story ends with a formative omission: will the Flying Fortress crash? That's left to our imagination. The pilot is still steering his wreck homeward.

Within the structure outlined above is woven some unobtrusive patterning. The boy's 'frantic | doggy-paddle' of the first stanza prefigures the boys' 'frantic waving' in the final stanza. And that 'waving' is part of a run of words which prepares us for the key action in the final line – 'waved back'. The poem moves through 'waving [...] waved [...] waving [...] waved back'.

The poem also waves towards a famous passage in book one of *The Prelude* where the young Wordsworth is bathing in the Derwent. This is the passage ('Was it for this') which began the 1798/9 two-book version of the *Prelude*. As the first poet-in-residence at the Wordsworth Trust and author of *In Wordsworth's Chair* (Flambard Press, 1995), Gerard Benson was well-versed in Wordsworth. In this poem, Wordsworth's 'naked Boy' and 'naked Savage' become 'naked boys'. As Gerard retells the story, he is also meditating implicitly on 'moral luck': why was it that he survived? The title 'The Bomber' brings in dilemmas of war, sympathy and retaliation. Although Gerard's lines approximate to Wordsworth's measure, blank verse, only roughly, he does deploy one line of regular iambic pentameter for the key event: 'A Flying Fortress lumbered into view'. The pentameter lifts this line and gives it might, even as the verb 'lumbered' carries the bomber's weight and woundedness.

'The real language of men'. The poem's 'waste-not-want-not' style foregrounds a possible excess in the last line. The poet could have written, simply and at the risk of bathos, that the pilot 'waved back'. Instead, he stretches it into the longer 'waved back at the naked boys on the Windrush bank'. Why? To me, the adjective 'naked' secures the allusion to Wordsworth mentioned above. The final word 'bank' completes a pattern in that the noun 'bank' now appears in every stanza. More importantly, the perspective shifts to the pilot looking down at the boys, which merges into the point of view of the poet looking back at his younger self. The poem circles back to its opening line in that word 'Windrush' into which is packed, I guess, an historic event from later in that same decade – the docking of the 'Empire Windrush' –which is what most of us now think of first when we meet the word 'Windrush'.

When a poem has the art of hiding art, we may examine its art all the more closely, even if that entails stating the obvious.

About the authors

alice hiller is a writer from London and Dieppe. She is the author of The T-Shirt Book (Ebury Press), and holds a PhD from UCL. Her journalism has been published in the *Observer* supplement and her reviews in *The Poetry Review*, *Poetry London*, *The TLS*, *Magma*, *Literary Imagination* and *Essays in Criticism*.

Rishi Dastidar's third collection, *Neptune's Projects*, is published in the UK by Nine Arches Press. He also reviews poetry for *The Guardian*, and is chair of Wasafiri.

Ed Reiss lives and works in Leeds. His publications include *Now Then* and *Your Sort*, which was shortlisted for the Aldeburgh Prize.

REVIEWS

by: Sarah-Clare Conlon, Lydia Unsworth, Lenni Sanders, Ian Pople, Edmund Prestwich, Belinda Cooke, Sally Baker, Kayleigh Jayshree

SARAH-CLARE CONLON

Lisa Robertson, *Boat*, 176pp, $21.95, Coach House Books

Anthony Vahni Capildeo, *Polkadot Wounds*, 100pp, £12.99, Carcanet Press

Janette Ayachi, *QuickFire, Slow Burning*, 66pp, £10.99, Pavilion Poetry (Liverpool University Press)

We might not always be able to judge a book by its cover, but in the case of *Boat* by **Lisa Robertson**, we can get a pretty good idea – a sail-shaped concrete poem (created by Canadian artist Kathy Slade) flags up that an experimental adventure lies ahead.

Robertson describes the latest iteration of *Boat* as "the accumulated record of a series of indexical readings of the sum of my quotidian notebooks", and explains that it includes "earlier records amidst newer ones". This process of using the charted waters of personal journals as a jumping-off point brings to mind Robertson's fellow Torontonian Sheila Heti's recent acclaimed Oulipian Fitzcarraldo tome *Alphabetical Diaries*, as does another autobiographical revisit, *My Life in the Nineties* by US poet and essayist Lyn Hejinian, who passed away in 2024.

Boat's maiden voyage was in 2001, with a second foray in 2009 and this latest exploration – sparked by lockdown in Robertson's now home France in 2020 and 2021 – making landfall in 2022. Earlier versions were published variously as the pamphlets and chapbooks *R's Boat*, *Rousseau's Boat* and *A Cuff*, and as contributions to publications including *Chicago Review* and *McSweeney's*. This expanded version includes eight sections, each with a distinct look and feel, yet each sharing a resemblance, with the effect of leaving the reader both at home as well as at sea.

While reading *Boat*, a book of poems, I was concurrently navigating (that sounds as if it's hard work – rest assured, it certainly is not) Robertson's equally experimental 'novel' *The Baudelaire Fractal* (Peninsula, 2023). There are similarities and crossovers in terms of themes (philosophy, feminism, flora and fauna, fashion) and also sometimes style, but each is very much not the other. As a structuralist, Robertson recognises this:

> Listen. The poetical work
> Neither forbids inexperienced sight
> Nor forgets their own mouth
> I fall between them
> An implement in its place.
> Structure is duty

and:

> There exists an obsession with structures that
>   dominate position

Robertson's work has a self-conscious, or perhaps, rather, self-aware quality. The writer questions the writer, the writer questions the writing. The meaning of writing, the act of writing, even the instruments of writing all come under scrutiny. As this is a notebook-based exercise, it's pleasing to see the notebooks get their own moment in the spotlight. In the section 'The Hut', a lined notebook is "a trellis", "pleached"; in 'The Tiny Notebooks of Night', "the ink changes from blue to black" in "the small sylvine notebook". Elsewhere the

The meaning of writing, the act of writing, even the instruments of writing all come under scrutiny.

notebooks are "soft pale-green medium-sized", "glossy persimmon-crested", "large creamy with title Precious Ego", "small blue-marbled with powder-blue cotton spine", "bought in London, December, 1999", "glossy black with red-ink-edged pages, water dampened" …

There's a level of confidence and perhaps, dare we say it, intellectual superiority – including numerous cultural references and callbacks to philosophers, painters, poets, the likes of Rousseau, Rimbaud, Plato, Goethe, Lucretius, Mallarmé, Dürer (mostly old blokes, it has to be said) – yet equally it's not without its chiding, verging at some points on self-contempt on the part of the poet:

[…] fretful self-important introspection […]
me with my asym   metrical concepts.

Asymmetrical is a useful signpost, both the word itself and this unusual rift. The new opening section, 'The Hut', is wrought in two by a gap, a ditch, a "centre seam", as Robertson describes it in her notes, perhaps purposely reiterated in the text thus:

I wanted to think into the   structure of appearances

This feature – device? gimmick? – both helps and hinders. In the example given just above, the break falls between words and seems to split the clause naturally; elsewhere (as in the earlier *asymmetrical* example), words themselves are sliced in two, with varying results. In some places, one 'normal' word becomes two equally 'normal' words, just in a quite new context; in some places, there's no rhyme or reason (apologies). Nonetheless, the stilted act it introduces to trying to follow the narrative in itself instils slowness and encourages close reading.

The other new section (both of "which select differently from the older notebook material, as well as from the past decade of newer notes") has a different look again. Leading into the close, 'The Tiny Notebooks of Night' is made up of a series of groups of three lines stepped and indented, creating a triangular leading edge reminiscent of a yacht's unfurled sail:

The weather fell across the pages themselves
    also across the mental image of the pages as I
        ]read them
        the wide margins and the sea-like
            monotony of typography

Meanwhile, the lines in the second section, 'Face', alternate between italics and roman to denote a kind of back-and-forth, while 'Palinode' is laid out as couplets, some even almost leaning towards rhyming (*rivets / secrets, create / escape, sequins / slowing*). These ebb and flow (as indicated by the book's Rousseau epigraph), creating a slightly off-kilter feeling, but one that's not unpleasant – if it's unfamiliar, you just need to give yourself time to find your sealegs.

Since the day I first set ears on **Anthony Vahni Capildeo**'s poetry, at a live event some time in the pre-pandemic era, I was mesmerised by its lilt and language. Reading it on the page is just as much a treat, and this latest full collection – possibly their ninth (correct me if I'm wrong, but they are nothing if not prolific) – is no exception.

Its title, *Polkadot Wounds*, appears as a phrase in the poem that opens the book, preface style. 'Summer, Launceston' (kind of rhymes with Branston, like the pickle) originates from Capildeo's stint as writer-in-residence in 2022 at the Charles Causley Trust's Cyprus Well, the Cornish poet's former home. It is inspired by Cornwall's once-capital's Norman castle ruins, "where stone runs / like honey", and the equally honey-hued wooden statue showing the injuries inflicted on local martyr St Cuthbert Mayne, in the church of the same name, as modelled on the cover.

Cornwall also seeps into 'Imaginary Gardens, for Sarah Cave' (editor at the county's independent publisher Guillemot Press) – "your church is covered with ramblers / roses mushrooming rucksacks" – and, possibly, 'Accusation Affirmation Woof Woof Woof' – "(there will be dogs in heaven)" (Capildeo's contribution to the Causley website mentions the mural in another nearby church depicting St Roche being brought bread by a canine crusader).

But Capildeo travels, and we have a fogged Mount Fuji

There's a level of confidence and perhaps, dare we say it, intellectual superiority …

on a trip to Japan, their home town of Edinburgh's "anti-slavery Greyfriars" (site of another famous pooch), black ice and Scottish dialect, the island of Ireland's island Inishbofin, and, of course, Trinidad, where the poet was born. 'Full-circle Bells, for Leila Capildeo' brings back the still painful memory of making or receiving calls from phones in communal digs, but with the extra jeopardy of those to Mama in Port of Spain being at the mercy of:

> the idea of earthquakes shatters up the stairs.
> Whales dive, chew through cable. Windstruck, as tree snaps wires.

This foreshadows, perhaps, the "mountain descending a staircase" of 'Purgatorio: Thirsty Work' (in the section 'Commedia', obvs), where the endless movement of the beautiful clear "mild waterfall" belies "tripping-places, drowning-places", and is emphasised in both repetition and typesetting:

> broadening into stairs of water,
>   flowing over rocks, broadening
>   to seating-places, limestone-mild.

Similar stepping appears in 'Outpouring', one of a few "afters" (there are also a lot of "fors") in the book, this responding to Zoë Skoulding's 2019 Seren collection *Footnotes to Water*, this in the initial section, which is entitled "Landskips" (a play on 'landscapes').

Wordplay is rife, and 'Fiddleheads' even refers to one of my favourite Capildeoisms, as regularly documented via their social media channels:

> nor one of my misreadings
> terroir/ terreur, blue / blur

See also "suffer / sulphur / soufflé" of 'Migraine Improv'. Their wordmaking is up there too – "monsterproportionate", "pleasecomeflying" (spotted in both 'Visit' and 'A Working Breakfast'), "the horizon's up-tipped" – and the imaginary collective nouns are original, funny and playful (try "an editorial of thunder and lightening" in 'Purple'). There are also riddles – "What am I?"; "When's a door not a door?" – and outright jokes, such as in 'Never Have I Ever':

> All neighbourhoods need
> a Utility Queer but I
> never was a dab hand with a
> toolbox. I'll kick any bucket. Takeaway my prayer,
>   make me the
> Neighbourhood Futility Queer.

Polkadot Wounds' third and final section, 'Gentle Housework of the Sacrifice', turns to transformations of self, serves up offerings and prayers, addresses queerness and transition ("bring up the girl without pink"; "I swear by my chromosomes / I'll be a decent brother"), faces the past to face the future ("Change this wherever-I-am / to a playground so I can / run away"), and affirms "My body is new with joy". Indeed, a joyous collection, full of fun.

Also based in Edinburgh is Scottish-Algerian poet **Janette Ayachi**, whose second collection *QuickFire, Slow Burning* was shortlisted for the Saltire Poetry Book of the Year Literary Award 2024 – her debut *Hand Over Mouth Music* won in what are recognised as Scotland's national book awards in 2019. Both are published by Pavilion: her first had a blue cover to reflect its watery themes; the follow-up, *QuickFire, Slow Burning*, appropriately is red.

> Fire is malicious.   It comes quickly
>   but extracts delight   in burning slowly.

So opens the titular poem, which jumps around on the page like the subject matter's destructive spread.. But as well as destroying whatever is in its path, fire can promote new life and growth and, as here, it can be symbolic of love, lust and all things relationships.

Ayachi explores all these aspects, elemental and environmental, and across the 23 poems, there are bonfires and fireworks, fire pits and cauldrons, gunpowder and cigarettes. There is fire as warmth and fire as light, with Norse memorials as "erect as candles" ('Disturbing

But as well as destroying whatever is in its path, fire can promote new life and growth and, as here, it can be symbolic ...

Graves') and mummified organs "placed back into the vault of the chest / like a candle in a moving lantern" ('The Mad Hatter of Heart Matter'). The language is fiery, too, and there is guttering and spluttering, while things are regularly engulfed and doused.

And as well as the flames licking these pages, we have many mentions of mouths, including, in one of the longer poems 'isolated, together', bitten lower lips, "Gauloises puffed pouts of French women", spitting stars and paper "eager to be tongued by my tentative inks". There's a nod to sculptor Dame Barbara Hepworth extinguished in the husk of her burnt-out studio, and, in 'Translating the Transcendental Mountain' (a commission for the Scottish Poetry Library), to Scottish Modernist writer and avid hill-walker Nan Shepherd "who listened / to the stream in surround sound". The effect is not just visual, it's almost tactile.

Other recurrences include references to winter and snowflakes and ice and Hogmanay – all a foil to the fire, although of course cold has its own ability to burn. 'Trees in Snow & Letting Winter Go' responds to paintings in the National Galleries of Scotland by French Realist Gustave Courbet, with "big beech trees smothered in icing / the first cake of an eager new wife" – her other half shows up a few lines later, when the tree roots are "like an ethernet cable unplugged / after no email from an absent husband". This same poem takes us to the land of fire and ice – Iceland – and closes, sparingly but effectively, with "I miss her like I miss the sun".

Volcanoes rise up more than once, as do earthquakes ('El Tremblor', the penultimate piece, binds woman to planet), alongside other seismic events, including the devastating harbour warehouse explosion in Beirut. There's a lot of international travel – we start and end in South America, taking in Brazil, Columbia and Panama along the way – there's also plenty of Edinburgh ("haunted Edina"), including Leith, Portobello and Stockbridge.

That leafy suburb features in 'Lobster', where people are pulled in towards a scene unfolding on the main thoroughfare "like kites on a string" (kites appear again, twice, in 'isolated, together'). Images are vivid throughout the collection ("televised ambulances / stretch across the screen / ball-gowned in sirens"), and language also takes the reader out of the ordinary: "analysis paralysis", "ceaseless seasons", "ash hush of a crematorium". Like Capildeo, there is a sense of fun when playing with ideas ("shavings / shredding / spherical" and "erosion / eroticism / miracle"), and although 'The Anatomy of Memory' warns that there's "a thin line between caring less / & becoming careless", fear not – care is in abundance here.

About the Author
Sarah-Clare Conlon's poetry pamphlet *Wanderland* is published by Red Ceilings Press in 2025. She has also written *cache-cache*, *Using Language* and *Lune*, a Poetry Book Society Winter 2023 Selection. Broken Sleep Books published her prose collection *Marine Drive*. She has been writer-in-residence at Manchester's Victoria Baths and Ilkley Literature Festival.

LYDIA UNSWORTH

Martina Evans, *The Coming Thing*, 88pp, £12.99, Carcanet
Katy Evans-Bush, *Joe Hill Makes His Way Into the Castle*, 84pp, £10.99, CB editions
Tim Tim Cheng, *The Tattoo Collector*, 72pp, £11.99, Nine Arches Press

"How did some people always know what to do, like?" pretty much sums up the heartbreaking inner confusion of Imelda, our narrator in *The Coming Thing* by **Martina Evans**, a long narrative sequence told in a series of prose-poem vignettes and set in 1980s Cork somewhere within the punk scene.

It's a man's world, scattered through with foreboding timepieces, eerily prescient band names and song titles, and women who appear to have figured something out but are unwilling to share it with Imelda, Evans's gorgeously naive narrator who tries her hardest In difficult circumstances to break through.

Abortion lies at the core of this collection, as at the core of a body. And this is a book very much about Imelda's body and its autonomy – who gets to choose its future, financially, societally, and how has Imelda's attention been primed to see and want certain things?

Abortion lies at the core of this collection, as at the core of a body.

With an overbearing father (referred to by first name only) and a mammy "who threw all her clothes in the river because she didn't want any more children. & then she died," Imelda's looking for a place that wants her, in which she can "be unbelievable too".

She's deftly contrasted with her friend Dora – stronger willed and independent – and the notion of distance is brought into question. How something can, to an onlooker, appear very easy to attain, but from within the struggling mind can remain worlds away. This therefore touches on class, sexism, and those casual forms of parental abuse that run rampant through many childhoods, and how those formative experiences affect the sizes and shapes of the worlds we imagine building for ourselves.

It's painful (and familiar) to witness Imelda's desperation navigating the highly volatile territory of talking about music, philosophy, or indeed having an opinion about anything. She's left in a chronic state of puzzlement. Even the desire for children is taken out of her hands (her boyfriend wants five, but she doubts if she does as she's been gently advised she's "too highly strung"). Evan's cleverly questions the *choice* involved in the freedom of abortion here with lines such as "No one asked me what I wanted & I was really hoping they would", "It's the grandmother who suffers most in these cases." (referring to the keeping of a child) and "I asked Carl if he thought it was right … & he said we'd paid now." There's a lifetime of being silenced here, of being told what to think and looking toward men for love and, in order to get that, trying to emulate what they might need. And Evans vocalises this precise type of silencing exquisitely.

Imelda's societal strangulation is implied in "the yellow necklaces of the city lights" of the Cork she's escaped to – an aptly chosen city name, it's suppressing something, it's waiting to pop, but will it ever? – and in frequent references to Ian Curtis, who "hung himself with a clothes horse," a domestic, beast-of-burden-esque item. In one moment of relief, Imelda is running, her "breath taste[s] sweet & sparkling, like red Tanora coming out of a bottle." A desire to not be contained.

The collection is replete with hollow containers: the dangerous womb; the "smell of the inside of an Easter egg"; a brooch, stood on, with its pearl popped out onto the floor.

In a scene of petty vandalism, into which Imelda is easily lured by the boys whose acceptance she seeks, her poor choices are framed beautifully as "hitting herself with her own brick." Poor Imelda seems to fluff everything – but what chance did she have?

"*Did you even know where you were?* said Dora when I said Murphy took us to a wild bit of the city. *It was another planet*, I said." Murphy appears as what might be the kind lad. There's an immediate attraction – he's styled as Imelda's *what if* – and of course she's never going to get him. And he won't get her either – he's not as pushy as the meaner lads. He hovers in the background of Imelda's more confident, more nurtured alternative (on another planet). This is the understated subplot of story, the nearness of a different future for Imelda, but one that nonetheless cannot be accessed due to the trappings of trying-to-please. It's done, as is the whole collection, with a very light touch, through snatches of dialogue and quickly disregarded thoughts and noticed details.

This is a book about the dangers of love, the dangers of needing it and of withholding it. In one staggering line near the end of the narrative, Imelda's father's eyes, his prison-state eyes, reappear – "his brown eyes like drinking chocolate" – still so sweet to the still-unloved still-child still wanting his affection.

The title of this collection not only refers to the internet and the patriarchal knowledge of the father, or to the abortion at the centre of the plot line, but also to the dreamy optimism of youth, ignorance, and the wildness of discovery. The future's coming, and it's full of promise and possibility, until it isn't. Much like life itself, for most of us, this is a tale of tiny tragedies, as incremental as the passing of time.

Katy Evans-Bush's *Joe Hill Makes His Way Into the Castle* launches us straight into some dystopic future where all the dreams we once had are on fire and in the centre of that fire is Kafka's Castle, unattainable

There's a lifetime of being silenced here, of being told what to think and looking toward men for love and, in order to get that …

as stable accommodation, caught in a maelstrom of broken promises, corruption, distraction, and the consequences of collective poor decision-making.

But there's hope here. From the "grey & gentle cradle of the past" we will raise our children ("our mighty atoms"), be them our own or simply the ideas that generate from the ideas which precede them. Either way, the next generation will "wreck our dusty curtains" and "trample our flowers before they can go out & spread their shine / In ways we never dreamed would be the ways."

Evans-Bush takes a very different approach to the father in Martina Evans's collection. There's no clinging to old ways here, no ownership of offspring. We're controlled perhaps, but we know it, and in that knowledge is revolution's seed. It's still a man's world – Evans-Bush is writhing in Kenneth Patchen's shadow, in the shadow of Joe Hill, of musician Leigh Stevens, Dostoevsky, and a host of disappointing male leaders – but she's found a use for it, a way to play with it, she's reappropriating their words and making it her own, she's making poetry.

Evans-Bush concedes she was low when she wrote *Joe Hill* ..., and through the exorcism that was the writing of these poems – the working one's way through tough times with a rule and some rigour (she cut-up lines of her favourite poet from her teen years, Kenneth Patchen, whom all the poems in this book are titled after, and then wrote her way out of their fragments) – she finds a kind of liberation or release. Reminiscent, in this way, of Joyelle McSweeney's *Death Styles*, emotions are pounded into submission, punched into new shapes.

There are moments of simple revolution amid the broader call for societal change. The acknowledgement that revolution begins in every relationship. As Evans-Bush says: "Each generation tries to break the chain" – that is, if we're lucky. Because inertia creeps, it's easy to be despondent, to be distracted, do nothing: "The dead don't mind us, we're just like them."

The collection as a whole swings wildly through emotions, back and forth like the swinging pendulum of binary politics. And if occasionally a little repetitive

and prosaic in its expression of anger, it doesn't make that anger any less important, and all the while the pages are shot through with killer, coffee-spit lines such as "Fuck your bunting" and "It was a bomby evening."

Frequent references to the colour grey hang low like brain fog. Birds soar over, crowds of sparrows shoot free, even their apparent escape from our humanly concerns exudes a kind of violence. We're always going to be in danger, that's part and parcel of being sentient, the uncertainty of our position: "the only evil / is doubt, it's said, and I am made of it."

Evans-Bush, sometimes quite overtly, as in poem #29 where she speaks directly to Patchen, is mining his lines like those of a prophet or elder for hope and guidance in the present moment. And sometimes she does find it. Such as in the lines "Be an eye, you say. We have to be alive / to every minute we're here," or where she seems to find calm, exhale, and accept each of our personal limitations: "because you can only begin from where you are."

And in that realisation is a beginning. Space for new hope to grow. Stop being jealous of the grass, the leaves ("so casual") and get on with it, "the genuine you [is] the one who was born with nothing to do but care." As Evans-Bush delicately ponders (and here I think of Martina Evan's Imelda again, want only the best for Imelda): "We are all, always & only, all of us children / & the promise we are given is always broken, / but what a promise! & so we love each other."

Tim Tim Cheng's narrator in *The Tattoo Collector* also finds herself living through a period of political and societal upheaval, this time in Hong Kong; and surrounded by shifting ideas of nationhood, she questions how to revolt, and more fundamentally how to become a person in such spaces. But where Evans-Bush claims "Art's not redemption. Art's just how we're tuned", it feels more redemptive here. Cheng finds inspiration in sculpture, in painting, photography, and in the more permanent fusion of one's body with the organic world, as afforded by the tattoo, and as detailed by the jellyfish tattoo that travels "from [her] spine all the way down

The collection as a whole swings wildly through emotions, back and forth like the swinging pendulum of binary politics.

[her] thighs" in a poem that closes with the lines "a marble marriage / with swirling tentacles."

The Pillar of Shame is discussed – a copper obelisk of contorted bodies by Danish artist Jens Galschiøt memorialising the loss of life during the Tiananmen Square Massacre of 1989, which was vanished in 2021 – and Cheng states "I preferred the pillar's absence. The outline of its base, a square lighter than its surrounding, spoke louder. Homemade palm-sized pillars spoke louder, too", implying that one way to deal with trauma is to adapt to it, to allow it to become a catalyst for change, and that one way to revolt is through art-making, to become an artwork onself. Elsewhere in the collection, she moves "to a country called writing" – the dissent, the freedom, here in refusing to be silenced.

Control is key, as evidenced by the first section's epigraph, attributed to Mei-mei Berssenbrugge: "A sense of being responsible for a crisis may also give a feeling of control." And you can feel the freedom this control gives bristling throughout the collection, navigating parents, grandparents, heritage, the changing status of Hong Kong, and the subsequent changing of the narrator, as she makes her own choices in given circumstances. "How lonely it is to choose" Cheng states in the poem 'Muscle Memory' – but how wild! This is poem as song, and song as nature, as animal, as birthright. The poem opens with the anthemic: "Courage is a half-rehearsed song. / You, you, you, you are the notes." It's all we can do to be alive, a sentiment that does echo Evans-Bush, and which we can only hope Miranda Evans's Imelda discovers in time.

Cheng says "To touch is to close the distance." – tattoos feature as a way of literally being touched by art, and also a way of using that art to tell a story, to make something beautiful from a world of fragments. Wounds feature – psychical, political – and are altered (redeemed) by art, by the tattoo. The topography of the scar is incorporated into the design, which, if successful, should "capture the skin's weather." The skin is a site of battle. This is a fully embodied poetics. Lines such as "longing is guttural" or "elation is neck-snapping" attest to the physicality of striving.

"Happiness comes like an ambulance / you hear from a distance" is one of my favourite lines in the book, the total fright of relaxing into something – the way it builds, overwhelms, and recedes again.

There are so many good lines in here I could quote out of context, from "mountains around you / are unnameable muscles" to "the colour / between black, brown, yellow, green / is called clarity" but what I enjoyed the most was how the collection weaves its way from the broad sweep of political happenings, through the inevitable pulls and tugs and drifts and regrets of being born into a family, to finally break out as a person boiling with agency.

It's nicely summed up in the following: "next to souvenir stalls, sick of / the millionth photo of one important leader / shaking hands with other important leaders, / we stop holding hands too." There's that courage again. The collection's penultimate poem, 'Hidden Agenda', whisks us through a club night, through a series of sentences beginning with the word *then*, with all the speed of booze-soaked evening, to finally end with the lines "then I am anti-elegy, / then I make –". And thus poetry arrives, storms out from the *I* like the blooming of wild flowers over the marked skin of circumstance.

Cheng finds inspiration in sculpture, in painting, photography, and in the more permanent fusion of one's body with the organic world ...

About the Author

Lydia Unsworth's latest collection is *Arthropod* (Death of Workers While Building Skyscrapers). Pamphlets include *These Steady Bulbs* and *Residue* (above/ground), cement,terraces (Red Ceilings), and YIELD (KFS). Work can be found in places like *Ambit, Banshee, Bath Magg, Blackbox Manifold, The Interpreter's House, Oxford Poetry, Shearsman, SPAM,* and *Tentacular*. Her forthcoming collection, *Stay Awhile,* will be published by Knives Forks and Spoons in 2026

LENNI SANDERS

Tom Jenks, *Melamine*, 56pp, £9, The Red Ceilings Press

Harry Man, *Popular Song*, 74pp, £11.99, Nine Arches Press

Kandace Siobhan Walker, *Cowboy*, 67pp, £11, CHEERIO

These three books, which I will discuss in order of recency, share some similarities: a feeling of alienation from aspects of modern society, and a great sense of inventiveness.

Published at the end of June 2024, *Melamine* is the fifteenth publication by writer and text artist **Tom Jenks**, excluding his collaboratively written work.

Red Ceilings Books chapbooks are exquisitely designed and very small, truly pocket size, but you get plenty of bang for your buck with *Melamine*, a book of untitled eight line poems that are full of brilliant turns of phrase and voltas that throw you off course. There's something very pleasurably destabilising in the way Jenks mixes together disparate tones, creating a continually surprising voice. Lines like 'Stay close, my hound' set you up and then go on to say 'and share your insights', knocking you down.

When I went to the launch event last September, Jenks said that as well as individual poems you could also interpret them as a sequence or as one long poem, which felt like an Easter Egg at the time, a bonus feature of the book that I hadn't yet discovered. But of course you can read the poems straight through in this way. They share similar themes, especially the world of work, with images of photocopiers and webinars. One poem ends 'You can make your demons work for you / if you can find an office small enough', followed by the next poem in the collection which opens, 'What would you think if this office was in space? / I think I would like it, I think I'd like it better'.

The modern world is something to escape; thwart and be thwarted by; or to cheekily undermine. Set against the drabness of the everyday, we have the landscapes of Arthurian legend or fairytales. We see 'ancient glades' and 'vanished kingdoms'. In one poem, the speaker addresses 'Noble Galahad, in your Fiat Punto' before moving to contrast him with 'Avon Lady', who suddenly seems like a much more Romantic character for her juxtaposition with the knight – a noble Lady of Avon.

The poems are full of puns and jokes – two good examples being 'I take no position, but I prefer lying down', 'The subtleties of his trousers escaped me / in a golf cart with a tiny goblin'. The way these jokes work feels like part of the same strategy of destabilisation that Jenks pursues when his speaker suddenly adopts a different tone or seems to shift priorities halfway through a poem.

Roughly a third of the way into the collection, the reader's attention is caught by the poem 'Bouncy ball, bouncy bouncy bouncy ball' which repeats the phrase 'bouncy ball' in a number of variations that alter how many 'bounces' the ball has before it. Both stanzas are nearly identical except for the final line in the second stanza: 'And so on'. The ending delights me – it creates a sense of a speaker describing the motion of a rubber ball to you, perhaps with deep boredom or perhaps with a kind of professorial interest, wanting you to completely understand the motion of the ball.

At the launch event, I was desperately hoping Jenks would read 'Bouncy ball' and very gratified that he did. Even more so than in the book, when read aloud it disturbs the poems around it. I can't even read it aloud alone in my living room without laughing. There is also close attention paid to sound. A line like 'Pumped up on beeswax, I fled the scene' is very satisfying on a sonic level, beginning with short sounds and urgent plosives before slowing down to 'beeswax', which then has a nice assonance with 'scene' at the end of the line.

There are often lines that echo each other's structure, creating a satisfying repetition or setting images against one another. Here's an example I really liked:

> I am Richard, the urban warlock.
> I am St Francis and I'm an absolute nightmare.
> I am Poseidon, king of the waves,
> but I'm not allowed near the vending machine

There's something very pleasurably destabilising in the way Jenks mixes together disparate tones, creating a continually surprising voice.

It really illustrates, I think, this poet's ability to raise questions that you know won't get answered, which is part of the pleasure of reading his work. *Melamine* is a great addition to Jenks' oeuvre.

Harry Man's *Popular Song* came out last April. This is the poet, translator and artist's debut collection, which combines lyric poems with more experimental forms.

One highlight for me was 'The Airborne Gooseberry Boy' which has a dense, pacey feeling to it, moving from character to character like a series of rapid cuts in a film – showing us the child speaker's interactions with teachers, doctors, priests, parents and grandparents, overwhelmingly figures of authority. It has an ominous, somewhat slippery feel, with moments of dark humour. At the doctors, the speaker chooses a sticker for being brave and says it looks like Skeletor but the doctor says it looks like Death. Then we get the excellent few lines:

> The doctor said
> I need to get big and strong so
> one day I could be like our friend, yes
> just like Death

Different forms in this collection included a N+20 version of 'I wandered lonely as a cloud' ('I water-skied lonely as a clownfish') and a poem that consists of onomatopoeias for the heartbeat from around the world ('Alphabets of the Human Heart in Languages of the World'). A large portion of 'Alphabets of the Human Heart' takes place in the footnotes, where Man lists the language of origin of each representation of the heartbeat as well as providing a translation for any that are also words. A short extract from the footnotes reads as follows:

> lab-dab – Telugu, pal-pal – Basque, pēng pēng – Chinese, Mandarin (also a cannon boom)

Another highlight for me was 'Who Dares Challenge Me? The President and CEO of the Company that Emits More Co2 than Any Other in the World's Statement on Third Quarterly Earnings Translated Using The Language of 90s Cult Boardgame *The Legend of Zagor*'. This poem combines two clashing tones to condemn this kind of corporation, in a way that is very funny:

> Despite economic uncertainty, our blood-curdling commitment through global underinvestment proves we can roll in the high hundreds consistently and grip a silver dagger over this once-peaceful land

Popular Song has a tendency to fill a poem to the brim with exciting words from a different lexicon, but sometimes I felt the poems were almost too full of these words, in a way that might inhibit the reader from fully experiencing the poem. This was more the case in narrative poems like 'Ground Truthing'. This poem about terraforming Mars ends with the fantastic lines:

> tonight we're off
> to see how far up he will go, when we throw Mitch high
> over the roof of the Excursion Module.

But by the time the poem reaches this point I'm already a little exhausted by the references to Solis Planum, Phobos, Echus Chasma and the like, but I realise this is a matter of personal taste.

'Night Meditation for Sleepless Birds of the British Isles' was a standout poem. It is full of the names of birds and body parts that are specific to birds, integrated into the poem in a really interesting way, slotting into lines and replacing what might have been there before, or could be imagined to have been there. This produces lines like 'Now it's time to take a deep buff-breasted sandpiper in / and let a deep buff-breasted sandpiper out' and 'As you meet the skylarks, mistle thrush closely.' The words become detached from grammar and meaning, distinct from the context they are placed in.

Popular Song is a really enjoyable first collection, full of warmth and wit and ideas.

Cowboy by **Kandace Siobhan Walker** was published September 2023. It is the debut collection from the

> *… sometimes I felt the poems were almost too full of these words, in a way that might inhibit the reader from fully experiencing the poem.*

writer, artist and film maker and was shortlisted for the Forward Prize Best First Collection that year. Many of the poems in this book address what it is to live under late capitalism, on and offline (with references to emails, to Instagram, browsing online and bandwidth). It has a highly distinctive, image-rich style.

Cowboy is infused with political energy, with one of the most exciting examples being 'Neopet', which takes a circular form to show the inescapable nature of the forces that govern our society. It begins ' – it's a circle, right? Virtual pet websites are about wealth accumulation' and ends 'And capitalism and its precedents are about wealth accumulation, which brings me back to–'. Another poem, 'Cleaning Ladies I' opens with:

> 'And we scream on the way to work, fuck working! We're flirting with the future on the nightbus. Between this job and the next.'

These poems weave in concepts and language from political and disability theory. 'Outlaw Sonnet' reminded me at times of Chelsey Minnis with its exclamation marks and its sense of luxury (images of the speaker 'dressed in ruffs'). It moves from 'apologies and / crip theory over coffee' to a description of the speaker 'reaching a critical mass of diagnoses' and continuing to 'keep living voluntarily'. In the last section, the poem tells us 'Ransom every kind of heaven and purgatory', ending (like 'Neopet') with a dash: 'like, we'll still / die, but at least-' The dashes might suggest that the poem is a moment of interruption into the order of things, which itself is interrupted – something else might speak over the defiant voice, but it will come back.

Walker's poems have a wonderful, snappy movement from one line to the next. Sometimes, in the poems with shorter lines, I'm put in mind of a detective speaking into a dictaphone:

> Masked in gateway fetishes,
> real people are modern fruit.
> Juice and paint, garden peas.

To me, these images sometimes have a loose and swirling, somewhat ungraspable quality.

At other times, the poems sometimes have such long, generous spilling-over lines that some of the poems are printed sideways. Along with the soft, matte paper of the cover, it makes *Cowboy* a tactile book to read, which feels fitting because of how vividly sensory much of the language is. For example, one poem, 'Mustang', talks about desire in a stream of synaesthetic images:

> For my stained glass mattress,
> we invent east, then west. Fuck, I'm chameleons about your lips, your sainted fingers.

There is something cinematic about both the voice and the images in these poems. Just after the line 'I play sad gay albums to a nub, summer grinds like a school dance' in 'Forest Gump', we get the following two lines that feel almost like film dialogue: 'I'm wise enough to know there are just two kinds of people: / girls with smudged mascara and girls with baby wipes'. And a poem with a similar feeling of making your way through the world, and finding your place in it, is 'Moon River' which opens with the line 'Party girls are art school drifters. Turquoise tea lights filled with menthol filters'. It sets the scene almost like stage directions at the start of a screenplay. These lines are also very beautiful in terms of sound – we have the half rhyme of 'drifters' and 'filters', and the repeated ts and fs at the starts of words in the second line.

These poems are highly musical and often wrap up with masterful closing lines that have a feeling of finality. The last line of 'Blue Pickup Truck' demonstrates both of these attributes: 'and I'm nobody's daddy in the baseball diamond.' Walker's first collection is captivating.

> *Walker's poems have a wonderful, snappy movement from one line to the next.*

About the Author

Lenni Sanders is a writer based in Manchester whose debut pamphlet *Poacher* was published by the Emma Press in 2019. Lenni's work has appeared in *Butcher's Dog*, *bath magg*, *Basket* and elsewhere, and she has reviewed for *The TLS* and *PN Review*

IAN POPE

Elisa Gonzalez, *Grand Tour*, 91pp, £10.99, Farrar, Strauss and Giroux

Victoria Chang, *With My Back To The World*, 101pp, £12.99, Corsair

Carlie Hoffman, *When There Was Light*, 67pp, £13.64, Four Way Books

According to the cover blurb of **Elisa Gonzalez**'s debut collection, Gonzalez 'dramatizes the mind in motion as it grapples with something more than an event.' The mind grappling certainly feels as though it is at the centre of these poems. There is something slightly relentless about the usually, short declarative sentences with their present tense verbs placed to the beginning of those sentences; this from the beginning of the poem, 'Roman Triptych,' 'Red stones piled in square towers. / Red roads cruise aqueducts. / Blue chain by the door / strikes a bell.' This is not a collection that ever feels as though it is going to catch breath; this feels like a younger poet in a hurry. And yet, Gonzalez puts three poems in this collection with the titles, 'To My Thirty-Year-Old Self', 'To My Twenty-Four-Year-Old Self' and 'To My Thirteen-Year-Old Self'. So, the title of the book, *Grand Tour,* not only references the kind of geographical education that the young upper-class male undertook in the eighteenth and nineteenth centuries; a 'grand tour,' that is referenced in the titles of some of the individual poems: Warsaw, Cyprus, Puente de Piedra, Gdansk. But the book, as a whole, seems to tip its hat to a kind of 'sentimental education', too. Overall, the dynamic of this book feels somewhat centripetal; the geography is pulled back towards the self experiencing, and it is a self explicitly delineated in Gonzalez's continual use of 'I.' The reader never feels that this 'I' is ever fictionalized; we are here, the 'I' tells us, embedded in the consciousness of Elisa Gonzalez.

A tension between the life lived and the mind reflecting on the living might also be seen in some of the poems' titles: 'Failed Essay on Privilege', 'Roman Triptych', 'Song of Experience, Epistemology of the Shower'. And yet, the book begins with two moving poems, 'Notes Toward an Elegy' and 'After My Brother's Death, I Reflect on the *Iliad*'. In both these poems, the rapid accumulation of detail conveys that sense of reaching for meanings in the aftermath of death. 'After My Brother's Death' begins,

'The water cuts out while shampoo still clogs my hair.
The nurse who swabs my nose hopes I don't have the virus, it's a bitch.
The building across from the cemetery calls itself
LIFE STORAGE.'

Those are Gonzalez' capitals. That eruption of detail at the beginning of the poem offers a disorientation which is followed by a move into the personal narrative,

'My little brother was shot, I tell the barista who asks how things have been,
and tip extra for her inconvenience. We speak only to the dead, someone tells me – to comfort, I assume, or inspire,

but I take it literally, as I am wont: even my shut up and fuck and let's cook tonight,
those are for you, Stephen.'

There is clearly an onward momentum in all the quoted lines; whether it comes from the mostly simple syntax, or from the onrush of detail, or the need to convey the narrative context of the writing. And the poems are designed to push momentum through those things; Gonzalez is nothing if not in control. Elsewhere there is more of a sense of lingering in a physical moment. In 'Fable', for instance, Gonzalez works her material in a slightly utilitarian, if more lyrical way,

'In the spring, ducks kick through reeds
spreading shore to shore on the unnamed pond.
The air reeks of ducks and thick, propagating reeds.

> *The reader never feels that this 'I' is ever fictionalized; we are here, the 'I' tells us, embedded in the consciousness of Elisa Gonzalez.*

The children in the house like to watch
from the window, though they turn afraid
when the ducks flock. Ducks nip at ankles and toes.
The mother and father let the reeds grow
without objection, and the pond greens and stinks
in the sweaty parts of summer
when no one wants to be outside.'

I've quoted that at length to show that Gonzalez is, perhaps, more interested in the children. The description of the ducks and the pond is a way of leading into the children's reactions. However, those more descriptive elements concentrate on the way the pond decays and the ducks are unpleasant and are clearly very different from the rather gentle creatures that the children might have encountered in books. The fable of the title reaches its climax towards the end when the children are given a pet duck and don't take care of it.

'So, you see the problem: what does it matter if [the
father] shoots
at the air, or the duck, or the deer
when the air is grayed like strands of hair
and the children will cry in any case
simply because they are children.'

The image of the air 'grayed like strands of hair' is not unusual in Gonzalez's writing. She tends to reserve the use of colour for moments of deeper emotion. In a later poem, 'Home', the mother and the two daughters plant flowers which are allowed to die in the dissolution of the parents' marriage and before they 'leave in the night,' In the final stanza, the narrator promises that 'to everything that's sad, I can add something that's happy.../The color of the water – I promise it isn't black, it's a pure unwasted yellow. / And the sun will come alive. /And the boats will come, too, circling under the sun.' There is an involving charge to Gonzalez book that is strong and achieved.

Victoria Chang is another FSG poet, but who is published in the UK by Corsair. *With My Back to the World* is her seventh book of poetry. Chang, like Gonzalez, is a poet of memorial, her 2020 book *OBIT* is a series of poems in the form of newspaper obituaries. And it is clear that *With My Back to the World* is a kind of memorializing, too. The book's title is taken from a painting by the American artist, Agnes Martin, who died in 2004. The Museum of Modern Art in New York comments that Martin's 'signature format [was] six by six foot painted canvases, covered from edge to edge with meticulously pencilled grids and finished with a thin layer of gesso.' And they quote Martin as commenting that painting was 'a world without objects, without interruption ... or obstacle. It is to accept the necessity of ... going into a field of vision as you would cross an empty beach to look at the ocean.'

Chang's poems seem to ventriloquise what the reader might presume to be the voice of Agnes Martin. Often these pieces are short prose paragraphs which start with a comment on Martin's artistic practice and then move into the artist's voice to comment on the way the painting might reflect life. If that summary suggests something bald and a bit obvious, Chang's exploration of that 'life' is, usually, neither of those things. This is the beginning of 'Untitled #12, 1981'

'Agnes must have wanted me to see innocence or
happiness when looking at this painting but all I see is
the gathering

of pink at the bottom. For every woman, there is a
man who is nearby. Every woman has asked a tree a
question. If you

ask a tree too many questions, it will fall down. You
can hear

a tree take its last breath, it sounds like gurgling. All
the answers are in the gurgling. A woman just shut a
window

because of someone staring in. I can't look at the
window

Chang's poems seem to ventriloquise what the reader might presume to be the voice of Agnes Martin.

without thinking man. Or kidnap. Or knife. I prefer the words of things I can't see, such as wind, now, exist.'

There is an undemonstrative quietness to this writing, that eschews lyricism in the style. The poetic lies in the movement of the thought. In this extract, the feminist 'charge', if we might put it that way, has its counterpoint in what Chang posits is the treatment of trees. We might see the treatment of women by men and the treatment of trees by humans as analogous, were it not for that movement into the violence of 'Or *kidnap*. Or *knife*,' and the gurgling death of the tree. Chang's poems are never precisely ekphrastic but are more a moving prism over Martin's paintings, perceiving them as sites for a powerful exploration of women's lives.

Carlie Hoffman's *When There Was Light*, is her second collection. It has a precise and delicate lyrical voice which might set it apart from the two previous collections. However, Hoffman, too, responds to the ways in which lives are lived among various social forces. And even where those social forces are colluding and dark, Hoffman's writing has an exuberance that always celebrates those the forces affect. This is particularly true of the Jewishness, and the lives of Jewish women, which Hoffman writes about with an affecting grace and precision; *When There Was Light* won the 2024 National Jewish Books Award for poetry.

The very strikingly titled 'While Waitressing at the Kosher Restaurant a Man calls Me a Whore and a Woman Rushes Behind Me into the Kitchen to Hand Me Her Baby', begins, 'Every season is good for killing girls, / the seaweed-black night foaming // with stars – a plaque of women's names.' There was a time when such an opening declaration would feel extravagant; its rhetoric part of someone's armoury. Today, I hope, we might see that differently. What Hoffman does, though, is to establish the night sky itself with the adroit delicacy of her description of that sky. Later in the poem, Hoffman writes, 'Every place that hurts you // is the season where the sun bursts / like salmon on fire.' These images are part and parcel of the exuberance of her writing. But the exuberance never feels forced or drummed up to serve some secondary 'poetic' purpose. There's a lovely effortlessness to Hoffman's writing which is deeply involving.

Part of that effortlessness is the ability Hoffman has to come up with the surprising metaphor, that never feels strained. This is the beginning of the similarly strikingly titled, 'Sundown, Looking at My Estranged Cousin's High School Yearbook Picture and All the Damage Done'.

'No moon tonight but the white bells of a woman's eyes squinting tacitly toward a camera, staring out

from the glossy page of a high school yearbook on a spring evening that stings like the elegy

of lifting a woman's hair from the shower drain, dredged deep
in the tiny, aluminium hold you hadn't scrubbed until now.'

The first turn the reader must take is around the 'but' in the first line. The phrase 'no moon tonight' doesn't actually witness the absence of the moon, in a sense, it establishes it as a reference point. So that when we move onto that image of the woman's eyes as 'white bells', we are almost ready for it, as strange as it might seem.

There is an element of synaesthesia in all this. How are eyes, bells? The poet creates the eyes as things we not only see but have an aural presence. In the next line, the eyes squint 'tacitly', two things which might also seem to have an inherent contradiction; the squint, voluntary or involuntary, but 'tacit' implying some kind of agreement, but with what? And as we move through the sentence, we have that very precise image of lifting the hair from the drain. But is it the woman whose picture stings, or is it the spring evening, or is it even the yearbook that stings. These floatings draw the reader in. And they draw the reader in to explore the world as Hoffman's title suggests, *When There Was Light*.

… even where those social forces are colluding and dark, Hoffman's writing has an exuberance that always celebrates those the forces affect.

About the Author

Ian Pople's *Spillway: New and Selected Poems* is published by Carcanet.

EDMUND PRESTWICH

Sasha Dugdale, *The Strongbox*, 88pp, £12.99, Carcanet

Imtiaz Dharker, *Shadow Reader*, 160pp, £12.99, Bloodaxe Books

Michelene Wandor, *Ergo*, 48pp, £8.00, Arc

Even on a quick initial reading, *The Strongbox* by **Sasha Dugdale** will take the reader's imagination in many different directions and offer immediate pleasures of many kinds.

First, it works on a remarkably broad canvas. Drawing on the myth of Troy and related ancient Greek material, it's epic in scale and effect in a way that develops from the work of Ezra Pound and other Modernist poets. Fragmenting the ancient Troy story, Dugdale rewrites incidents from it in anachronistic ways and mashes them up with incidents from other stories in a range of scenarios. Already in the first section – 'Anatomy of an Abduction' – we see the special kind of breadth this gives: a rain of vivid glimpses of domestic life, domestic violence, war, flight, seduction, abduction, rape, sometimes in nineteenth, twentieth or twenty-first century incarnations, sometimes in a Homeric one, sometimes hovering between, as when a soldier sent to collect a girl – perhaps Helen of Troy, perhaps a modern trafficking victim – drives past bullet-holed road signs but carries a bow. Breadth, then, is partly a matter of historical range, partly a matter of emotional variety. The poet moves us from scene to scene with a speed that I would call dazzling except that the scenes we move between are so solidly and clearly established in themselves. This combination of speed and clarity depends on the vivid economy of Dugdale's images and the sureness of her rhythms. What makes it moving is the quiet empathy with which she presents many of her characters, and the way humble lives, sometimes caught in devastating circumstances, are given weight by the epic context and style of various sections.

The impression of breadth and scale also comes from Dugdale's virtuoso handling of different forms. There are fourteen numbered sections, varying in length from one to nineteen pages. Most are in verse, sometimes rhyming, sometimes not, but II, IV and VII are short drama scripts in prose with stage directions. II – titled 'In the Rehearsal Room' – is a brilliantly comic dramatic monologue, spoken by a patronisingly self-satisfied theatre director presumably putting on a play about Troy. VII, a stage or screen passage in which Helen tells her dreams to a bored, then jealous Paris, is equally funny. It's more haunting than II, though, because other tones are interwoven with the satire, glimmers of wistful yearning and (this being a dialogue, not a monologue) a frustrated desire for communication on Helen's part. This section, in other words, is much more layered than the second. For readers of ancient Greek literature, there's even an apparent allusion to one of the most poignant moments in Pindar's victory odes.

Dugdale works by presentation, by showing, not telling, in the old phrase, letting us arrive at our own responses to the images and scenes she conjures. Her approach to imagery is itself highly varied. Her pictures are often powerful in a literal way, vividly presenting a situation that's significant in itself and seems to represent some kind of archetype of human experience or behaviour:

> She's told not to open the door
> so she huddles, draws her furred hood tighter
> the chill of leatherette under her thighs
> smell of petrol from jerrycans

They can create metaphors as startling as this comparison of the gods to dogs:

> *gods weave around each other*
> *barely touching*
> *sniffing one another's genitalia*
> *saying nothing*

Or they can plunge us into surreal fantasy:

> *Death came to the plain and perched in a tree*

The poet moves us from scene to scene with a speed that I would call dazzling except that the scenes we move between are so solidly and clearly established in themselves.

She wore a riding habit with puffed sleeves
Her shoulder blades were a pattern of kohl-
ringed eyes

It seems clear to me that The Strongbox is a major work that will repay endless revisiting. Line by line, phrase by phrase, word by word, the writing ripples with invitations to reflection. With rereading, as well as thinking more deeply about the major structural continuities, one starts to absorb multiple tiny echoes that are themselves fresh triggers for thought, like the echo between the description of Death in the last section I've quoted and the description of someone who may be Helen or may be a modern, trafficked prostitute 'bawling her eyes out, kohl / marking her cheeks' in section one.

Many, even most of the poems in **Imtiaz Dharker**'s Shadow Reader present some form of suffering, cruelty, oppression or abuse. However, they don't cloud our impressions of these things by pushing the poet's own emotions at us; presenting scenes and situations in a gently understanding way, with a polished musicality of sound, they let the beauty or cruelty of what they show speak for itself, in all its subtlety of nuance and overtone. In other ways, they're highly varied in style and imaginative mode. Some offer what appear to be direct accounts of literal events, letting broader metaphorical or representative suggestions shine through by implication; some, at an opposite extreme, are like pieces of fairytale or myth; many include elements of both. The lovely 'For the Girl on the Elizabeth Line' is an example of the first mode. Its language seems simple and transparent, achieving power by a sudden deepening of tone in lines three to five:

Standing by the door
the way young people do,
as if a seat is a waste
of life, you are lost

in each other.

Only in the third stanza does it emerge that what we're seeing isn't the scene of joyful young love it seems at first glance. The whole poem reverberates with complex suggestions of power, oppression and helplessness, both in the couple and in the passengers who silently watch them. The way our understanding of the couple's relationship changes is a wonderfully delicate evocation of how liable we are to misinterpret our fleeting glimpses of other lives. At an opposite extreme, formally speaking, we have the sonnet 'For the Woman Who Changed Back to a Snake'. Addressed to the woman / snake by someone who may be her mother, this poem seems to create an original, profoundly ambiguous myth related to the myth of Persephone and folk tales of the selkie or seal woman. Its vivid, highly wrought language makes a series of intensely sensuous imagistic impressions so that on one level it's very concrete. It might be called abstract on another because we can read such very different stories into the chain of metaphors. These stories converge to suggest ideas and feelings about female beauty and the habitual mistreatment and proper respectful treatment of women in a way that's the more powerful and the more wide-reaching for being indirect. There's a tragic interpretation by which the daughter addressed can only escape abuse by dying. Here's the sestet:

They can say you vanished. You made the choice
to fall into the earth's waiting arms
and find the tongue you lost, your silenced voice,
away from man's narrow gaze and casual harm,

back to the place that calls you goddess, queen,
and shivers at the power of your skin.

That sends shivers down my spine. So much is happening, such huge forces seem to collide within the gravely measured lines. For example, in a reading that links this poem with 'For the girl whose hair escaped' – perhaps inspired by the famous case of Mahsa Amini, whose murder by Iran's morality police sparked such widespread protest – there's contempt for evasive

The whole poem reverberates with complex suggestions of power, oppression and helplessness, both in the couple and in the passengers who silently watch them.

authority, respect for the woman's strength, pity and indignation at the repression of women's voices, joyful awe at the power of female beauty when properly seen, and SO MUCH MORE.

Such explosive concentration and absolute commitment to a mythic-metaphorical approach is unusual, even unique in the book. However, vivid, occasionally surreal images appear quite frequently, complementing the more transparent techniques of sympathetic observation. Another essentially metaphorical poem, 'Out of the rose garden', opens with the mysterious lines, 'When you come away from the rose garden / your eyes have changed colour in the rain'. One of my favourite poems that works essentially and startlingly by metaphor is the savagely beautiful, untitled three liner,

> But the roses are savages
>   that will eat you
> alive, given the chance.

This is a volume that weaves together a number of separate but related concerns and creates a quiet interplay between them. The lighter textured, more explicit poems are important in the total economy of the work because they make it easier to read across between poems and areas of preoccupation. The central focus is often broadly moral and political, but concern with the relations between people as individuals, as members of one or another gender, one or another class or religion, are seen in a wider context of nonhuman life and of mortality, the whole being framed by recurring references to a youthful Dharker's early visit to a fortune teller or 'shadow reader' who predicted the year of her death, supposedly the year of composition of the book.

As in other Dharker's other books from Bloodaxe, the writing is amplified by her own fine black and white drawings.

The wide canvases of *Shadow Reader* and *The Strongbox* embrace many lives, some sharply realised as individuals, others sketchily included in panoramic views. In this way, both books offer many of the satisfactions of fiction in a concentrated and distilled form.

Michelene Wandor's chapbook *Ergo* represents a very different poetic. My general sense is that moving from Dugdale's and Dharker's books to hers is like turning from oil paintings – crowded, impasto canvases in *The Strongbox*, more thinly layered ones in *Shadow Reader* – to an album of delicate, almost transparent, semi-abstract watercolours. Most of her poems are very short and all use minimalist imagistic techniques to hint at emotions, narratives and situations in a way that's often almost ethereally bare of human presence. Even a poem called 'song', which does invoke images of physical intimacy, does so in a rarefied, discarnate way:

> scroll down the side of your face as you leave
> remember the eyes' intrigue, the accidental promise
> of a hand's brush
> the shape of lips curved into a smile
>
> leap in, soft, caressing, taste
> the warmth of words, the ebb
> and swell of an unmeasurable caesura, with
> no time for now
>
> in this moment of departure
> someone
> has taken all your notes

Every idea, every impression here seems to dissolve as it forms. Line 5, the most active and sensuous in the poem, suggests a cat, not a person. Gaps in punctuation visually blur the contours of the syntax, and sometimes create real ambiguities. Even where the syntax seems clear, meaning can be hard to make out with confidence. In the first line, for example, how do you scroll down the side of a face, except if it's a picture on a computer screen? Is the poem about the end of an affair (various elements seem reminiscent of Eliot's exquisite 'La Figlia Che Piange')? Or is it about writing, or perhaps sculpture or painting, as lines 3 and 4 suggest? I can't define its subject, which seems to me to hover between possibilities, to slide between different orders of experience, but it creates impressions of beauty,

Every idea, every impression here seems to dissolve as it forms.

tenderness and regret that are the more haunting for not being fully graspable.

The distinctive beauty of these poems seems to me to depend on two things; the harmonious flow and sensitive patterning of their sounds and the combination of vividness and elusiveness in the imagery. More than pointing out to the surrounding world, they induce a dreamlike state focused on the movement of the mind between the impressions forming and reforming themselves within it. Here's the first half of 'vulture':

> vultures in the distance are dark
> butterflies
>   a moment of delicacy, wheeling into
> a flower, a winding road above our heads

About the Author
Edmund Prestwich lives in Manchester and taught for many years at the Manchester Grammar School. He is the author of two collections and reviews poetry for several magazines.

BELINDA COOKE

Marie Howe, *What the Earth Seemed to Say: New and Selected Poems*, 97pp, £14.99, Bloodaxe Books

Grace Wilentz, *Harmony (Unfinished)*, 61pp, €11.99, Gallery Press

Marie Howe's *What the Earth Seemed to Say* is an intense, mindful mix of the spiritual and sensual, evolving from a back story of sexual abuse inside and outside the home: 'he [her brother] barely hears the springs of my bed when my father sits down –' ('The Attic'); 'A gang of boys. They pulled the heavy garage doors down, / and tied us to them with clothesline' ('Sixth Grade'). Combine this with heavy-duty bible-based Catholicism and the stock advice to 'show not tell' is taken to an altogether new level, revealing a poet unlike any other. Now past seventy, though long lauded in the USA, it is hard to comprehend (hats off here to Neil Astley) that she is being published in the UK for the first time.

The epithet 'half nun, half whore', assigned to Anna Akhmatova by Stalin's culture minister, Andrey Zhdanov fits equally well the religious and sexual polarities of this collection. Head for the best wine first, skipping the mellow, reflective, dog lover *New Poems* (2023), for the mind-blowing immediacy of the *The Good Thief* (1987) – fears of dying will feel like sleepwalking after the concrete physical tightening and Shakespearean-style suggestions of death as the bridegroom of what we get here:

> Nothing will ever reach this deep. Nothing will ever
>   clench this hard.
> At last (the little girls are clapping, shouting)
>   someone has pulled
> the drawstring of your gym bag closed and tight.
>   At last
>
> someone has knotted the lace of your shoe so it won't
>   ever come undone.
> Even as you turn into it, even as you feel yourself stop,
> you'll whistle with amazement between your residual
>   teeth oh jesus
>
> oh sweetheart, oh holy mother, nothing nothing ever
>   felt this good.
>   ('Death the Last Visit')

Each lived second is dissected with all nerves exposed – what if Eve had not acted: '… like the moment when a bird decides not to eat from your hand, and flies, just before it flies,' ('Part of Eve's Discussion'); how would the Virgin Mary have felt at being chosen?:

> – I was blinded like that – and swam
> in what shone at me
> …
> only able to endure it by being no one and so

The epithet 'half nun, half whore', assigned to Anna Akhmatova by Stalin's culture minister, Andrey Zhdanov fits equally well the religious and sexual polarities of this collection.

specifically myself I thought I'd die
from being loved like that.
   ('Annunciation')

And who would opt for such an unusual object poem – a meadow as extended writing metaphor: 'As we walk into words that have waited for us to enter them, / so the meadow, muddy with dreams, is gathering itself together // and trying, with difficulty, to remember how to make wildflowers.' ('The Meadow').

This searing almost visionary engagement with the immediate world stems from God and the devil as permanent companions from her earliest memories. Here, with hints of a dark humour, her dark side surfaces as an obsession with scissors:

   I longed
to throw them out, but how could I get rid of something

that felt oddly like grace? It occurred to me finally
that I was meant to use them ...
   ('What the Angels Left')

while in 'The Split' we meet her mischievous, sacrilegious secret friend: 'She'd start the fires under the bed. / I'd put them out'; 'She was mean and she liked it ... / Mean as she was, I miss her.'

But it is the loss of her brother to Aids and many further others, that has led her to accepting death, paradoxically, as an affirmative reinforcement of the joy of living: 'Often, I'm lonely. / Sometimes a joy pours through me so immense.' ('Magdalene Afterwards'). Think John Cleese in *Clockwise*, 'I can stand the despair. It's the hope!' as her dying brother tells her: 'Soon I will die, he said, and then / what everyone has been afraid of for so long will have finally happened, // and then everyone can rest.' ('The Cold Outside'). While the superb standalone lyric 'Sorrow' movingly suggests how we grow through grief after all the uncertainty:

So now it has our complete attention, and we are
made whole.
We take it into our hands, like a rope, grateful and tethered,
freed from waiting for it to happen. It is here, precisely as we imagined.

For Howe, losing her brother has been like losing her other half, harrowingly caught by way of a dramatic monologue: 'In daylight, 'every tree became you. / And pretending, I kissed my way through // the forest, until I stopped pretending / and stumbled, finally here.' ('Gretel, from a Sudden Clearing').

What the Living Do, (1998) focused specifically on their last days together, covering every gamut of emotion as they exchange views on death, often with a shared sense of humour – his response when she says she loves him like a life partner: 'Maybe you better start looking for somebody else' ('One of the Last Days').

This is such a rich gathering, one can hardly do it justice. Her collection *Magdalene* (2017) is praised for drawing on Mary Magdalene's life to look at every aspect of women's experience, and, in general, her spirituality stands outside of any dogma. But, nevertheless, throughout she is the ultimate poet seer suffering and loving in God's world at a supersensual level – here, to conclude, lines from her most quoted poem:

... This was eternity, when
nothing happened that wasn't

already happening. She couldn't remember.
After the burning, even the light went quiet.
She didn't think God would be so

specific, so delicate – inside her elbow, under
her arm, the back of her neck,
and her knees.

It's true she struggled at first, until after
the breaking. then God was with her, and she was with him
   ('Encounter')

This searing almost visionary engagement with the immediate world stems from God and the devil as permanent companions from her earliest memories.

The New York poet **Grace Wilentz** became an Irish citizen in 2015 after arriving in 2005 to study the Irish language. Accolades for her first collection *Limits of Light* (2020) established her Irish reputation. Now, *Harmony (Unfinished)*, takes us through the joys and fragilities of this new life: 'I didn't know / if I was paralyzed or revitalized … // But in that cold, opaque sea, somehow I started treading water / and hand on heart, I never felt so Irish.' ('The Forty Foot'). This coincides with love lost and gained, and onto being more comfortable in her own skin: 'I know / how to keep my feet mostly planted // resisting the undertow's / familiar tug.' ('Beaches, Then and Now'). As a result, there is a more relaxed readiness to convey the mindfulness of the collection's epigraph of the sixties' poet Jack Gilbert, 'Why not the life?' Tightly-structured, well-honed language – albeit not using traditional forms – begins with intriguing shifts in perspective to reinforce the disorientation of her new life, and on to poems with the solidity of artefacts to give an immediacy to nature and art from her travels in Brazil and in Dublin.

She sets out with poems on that citizenship threshold. Having now lost both parents, 'Home House' reflects on her lost identity as she sits in her interlocutor's home literally 'holding the baby.' The poem's insider/outsider perspectives are reminiscent of Elizabeth Bishop's approach, here subtly interweaving tentative feelings of belonging, and hypothetical imaginings of motherhood – note, also the physical immediacy of that 'small weight':

> I was never here before, of course.
> What I mean is being in a home house of my own.
> Here, on the inside you don't look out,
> don't have time, the way looking in you do.
> My arms were like a circle. I sank into the sofa
> and the small weight of the boy in my lap
> became a part of me till I didn't feel him anymore,
> or the holding
>   ('Home-House')

In 'The Forty Foot' she also shifts the focus between the queue of swimmers waiting to jump from Dublin's famous promontory, to the queue in the immigration Centre: 'Each time the sea licked the step / the cold shocked me to my core.' Here, she includes a bit of her dark humour on a friend on the same path: 'knowing what it meant to her to have her status not tied // to a husband who tried to run her over twice.' 'Shadowboxing' is a clever extended metaphor to reinforce her uncertainty of the unknown, with a thought-provoking open-endedness to the implications of 'shadow':

> I feel I've been here forever, swinging,
>
> perpetually in training for meeting
> what seeks me out in other realms.
>
> I shuffle or dive and my opponent
> falls to pieces in shadow.
>   ('Shadowboxing')

The collection's middle section takes us to a stay in Brazil coinciding with a settled relationship, touchingly and precisely caught: 'Waking with the tip of my nose / so close to a soft neck / with its delicate ridge of spine –'. It feels like she is at home at last: 'as if I'd lived a thousand lives / and in this one somehow forged / something beautiful out of a lot of bad luck.' All in all, it really captures the comfortable ordinariness of a loved life:

> At that hour I'll find myself here again
> as we make dinner side by side, a song
> quietly playing in the background,
> chopping beside steaming pots
>
> of rice and beans and sharing a cool beer,
>   ('Gift of the Magi')

And with this, comes the luxury to just enjoy life, evidenced in: more love poems, reflections on how she has changed, and sharing Brazil's landscape and

Having now lost both parents, 'Home House' reflects on her lost identity as she sits in her interlocutor's home literally 'holding the baby.'

culture with the reader. A real gem is the ekphrastic poem 'Interior with Girl Reading', a painting by Henrique Bernedelli, where we see Wilentz's economic crafting at its best – one can almost hear the silence:

> Like a last song, this quiet moment
> where one high window filters
> light to four walls –
>
> here is the dream, elapsed.
> From the creased sheets
> yesterday's lines
>
> sing with clarity
>
> as set down by a mind
> that hungered for silence.

The collection's final section has us mainly back in Dublin, where her love of art and a particular interest in stained glass dominates. Here her eye for concrete detail and strong sinuous language really comes into its own: 'Sash windows with their hidden / lead weights perfectly balanced / for the hand to close without strain', 'Blue slates cut from the quarry, /sliced and graded' ('A True Record'). Throughout, Wilentz writes with a real respect for language and craft leaving you with poems that you almost feel you can hold in your hand.

About the Author
Belinda Cooke is a Russian translator and poet with seven books to date. Her most recent include a prose memoir on her mother's life: *From the Back of Beyond to Westland Row: A Mayo Woman's Story* (2023) and the poetry collection *With Our Own* (2024) on the diasporic experience, both from The High Windows Press.

SALLY BAKER

Amanda Dalton, *Fantastic Voyage*, 68pp, £12, Bloodaxe Books

Rebecca Watts, *The Face in the Well*, 63pp £11.99, Carcanet Poetry

Victoria Gatehouse, *The Hawthorn Bride*, 76pp, £14, Indigo Dreams Publishing Ltd

As an exploration of different aspects of the self, **Amanda Dalton**'s 'Fantastic Voyage' journeys through time and space, inner and outer worlds. It is a jam-packed, bumper collection made up of several different parts, including a long central poem, 'Notes on Water', and is bookended by two 'Fantastic Voyage' title poems providing entry and exit points for the journey in the pages between.

Reading the collection feels to me a bit like a trip to the funfair, where you try out all the different rides and experience a wide range of emotions. It begins in childhood, travels through loss and grief, to illness, losing and searching for a sense of self. The layers of a life are examined, with a variety of voices documenting the process of discovery. Imaginative elements are interwoven with dreams and memories. It is entertaining, theatrical, visual and sensory, exhilarating and disorientating, as well as poignant and moving. The poems are rich with colour and imagery. Although at times the journey becomes difficult, I feel I am in safe hands, expertly guided through unknown territory.

The title of the first section, 'Look Inside!' reminds me of those origami fortune-teller games from the school playground, where you lift a flap to reveal your future. Fittingly, it is followed by a series of prose poems, each with an unsettling narrative, some suggesting possible destinies. They include tales of horror, myth and folklore. These poems feature a six-foot tapeworm, the probability of a swallowed apple pip growing into a tree in someone's stomach, and the phenomena of spontaneous combustion. These are all stories I remember hearing as a child. One poem mentions Matilda Rooney, 1885, of whom it was said 'All that was left were her feet.'

A central narrative poem, 'Notes on Water' is a kind of dream sequence written in two parts. It documents the illness and subsequent death of a partner, through interwoven voices, one an internal

Reading the collection feels to me a bit like a trip to the funfair, where you try out all the different rides and experience a wide range of emotions.

stream-of-consciousness 'I', and the second a more factual 'she'. There are watery images throughout. The narrative describes the process many people go through in grief, searching for ways to understand events, piecing together details to try to make sense of loss. Descriptions of inner and outer worlds effectively convey a sense of detachment and disorientation as well as intense emotion. I particularly like the long list, made as a distraction while walking by a sea loch, of 'everything she saw – ' here is just part of it:

> 'a Tennant's lager can, marsh marigold in clumps, 8 oyster-catchers, 14 adult sheep, 9 lambs, a broken rowing boat, a pair of dark-coloured ducks with 6 young, a crow, ringed plovers (5), red plastic –

The poem moves back and forth in time and place, seemingly adapting to a new reality, where water has altered the familiar landscape and everything has shifted.

In the final section, 'Haunts and Apparitions' poems explore the body, illness and vulnerability. 'Ten Signs of Possession', a series on unusual physical phenomena, echoes the first section in its strangeness. There is an overarching theme of feeling or being lost and of acclimatising to a new reality, as in 'Missing', where:

> We were looking for a woman in blue
> when I wore red, looking for a quiet, bespectacled spinster when I was roaring

and also, in 'The Possibility of Fog':

> though it's only 2pm, if I can be so suddenly
> and spectacularly lost in the place I was born

In 'The Vegetable Lamb of Tartary', there is a strong sense of *before* and *after*, adjusting to a different way of living, with an uncertain future:

> and I wonder if this is how we'll live, if we live
> at all: scavenger-hunters, doors lying open

onto dark, the world returned to trees?

This collection is a voyage of discovery, of loss and the tentative beginnings of recovery, with the body as a vehicle of travel. It is rich and full of life.

The poems in *The Face in the Well*, **Rebecca Watts**' third collection, are often formally structured, using syllable counts, repetition and rhyme schemes. This patterning feels like neat embroidery, a sampler stitched together using various techniques to create a bigger picture. At first glance the individual poems seem delicate, beautifully crafted, and they are. But their formality often contains a fierceness within the language which threatens to break through the surface, a desire perhaps to push the boundaries. In 'The Landscapes of my Childhood', she begins 'The landscapes of my childhood were cosy', suggesting a sense of order and neatness. As an adult however, there is a wish for this comfortable domestic backdrop to be disrupted:

> I'd like to arrive in the landscapes of my adulthood –
> to feel precarious, scared even, at where I've come to

A host of 'real' wild animals – 'gorillas, elephants and giraffes' are invited into the poem, where, in the changing environment of adulthood, 'the flora abounds, very hungry, and grows huge'.

This sense of wanting to escape from an orderly, well-mannered environment seems to be a recurring theme. The title poem tells the story of a cautious child, who, after being warned of the danger of wells, is initially obedient. One day however, she risks looking into the water. The reflected self is the same, but somehow *other*:

> Rough brick grazed my palms as I leant over the side,
> strained on tiptoes to peer into the gloom,
> where I recognised a face, like mine but changed –

Something magical happens when the face appears, revealing another self who seems to be free from ordinary human emotions:

This sense of wanting to escape from an orderly, well-mannered environment seems to be a recurring theme.

at home deep down, connected to the source, needing a reflection to make it live.

The Alice-in-Wonderland quality discovered in the mirror-universe of the well, chimes with some of the collection's repeated motifs, where childhood stories and mysteries are explored, along with actions and consequences. I particularly like the series of 'Soundings' poems threaded through the pages: four short poems reflecting on childhood memories. In 'Soundings II: Waiting for Mary Poppins', the world makes sense: 'Rules and cleanliness/are all we want'. But sadly, in a later poem 'The Great Disappointment', Mary Poppins has left and will not be replaced, leading to the realisation 'that perhaps we'd only dreamt her'. Poets and writers also feature in these poems, including Emily Bronte, whose favourite task, we discover, is ironing. Liberating herself from home, the usual site for 'women's work', Emily's iron enters 'a wet and heavy land//through which a burning body moves, /directed by her hand'. In the final image, Emily satisfyingly folds up the world like a tablecloth.

Various animals feature, sometimes dead, as in '"Disposing of dead rodents is a man's job" (Mumsnet Forum)' where 'a rat the size of her head' is ceremoniously wrapped in bin bags. Other animals are on the point of extinction, as in 'The Wandering Albatross', or serve as symbols, as in 'Song', where 'Dolphin is the soul/ before the world gets to her'. Among representations of cosiness and safety, it feels that at any point the landscape could become rewilded, with feral creatures around every corner. Despite all our rules and manners, she seems to suggest, some of the wildness out there will inevitably make its way into our own bodies, perhaps via the compost heap in 'Om':

so there's a hint
of rat and snake
in all of us

Playful, and with a sharp wit, these poems reveal that despite our apparent domestication, we are still close to animals in many ways.

Various animals, whether domestic, wild, or in captivity, also feature in the pages of **Victoria Gatehouse**'s collection, *The Hawthorn Bride*. Her first full collection, it is accomplished and assured, with linked themes running through. It reads as a conversation with the natural world, placing domestic life and nature side by side, so they merge and interrelate. Many of the poems are gentle ecopoems, giving a voice to elements of the natural world. Others are inspired by fairy tales and folklore, while some weave 'stranger than fiction' scientific facts into their lines. There are moments in nature stolen from a busy life: juggling roles, in between the school run, in the kitchen, or out in the world. There are poems about family members, dogs, zoo animals, amphibians, snails, as well as a host of unusual or strange women. Amid the gentleness, there's often a kick – knives, flashers, death and dying, blood and killing, always just under the surface, as in nature.

Trained in Zoology, Gatehouse weaves scientific detail into her narratives, successfully combining fact and fiction. There is an awareness of the seasons and the Celtic calendar of solstices and equinoxes, beginning with the title poem 'The Hawthorn Bride', which references the May festival of Beltane, with its themes of blossoming and fertility:

Imagine
what it would be to cup her heart
a yellowhammer in a grotto of thorns

This is one of many natural metaphors effectively used in the collection to illustrate feelings. The line 'a foretaste of what's to come' invites the reader in and this poem skilfully manages to kickstart the collection with a burst of energy. Threaded through the book are a series of poems about trees from the Ogham alphabet, an ancient Celtic alphabet where each letter is represented by a tree or plant. These poems provide a framework for other poems to fit within.

Some of the titles alone make me want to read these poems: 'Darwin's Daughter and the Stinkhorns',

Amid the gentleness, there's often a kick – knives, flashers, death and dying, blood and killing ...

'Pornography for Pandas', 'Smoking is Not Normal for Orangutans'. These last two, based on true stories about zoo animals, walk the tightrope between being funny and heartbreaking. We meet Shirley, a young adult orangutan in rehabilitation after learning to smoke:

> her agile hands, grown proficient
> in gathering lit butts from concrete

There are so many different perspectives and experiences explored in these pages, a richness created through unusual and diverse voices. The mix of strong, impactful poems alongside those that are quieter makes for a good texture overall. I like the gentleness in many of the nature poems: the beautiful imagery and sensory description working together to immerse the reader in the environment. The occasional sharp wit, along with the contemporary language and everyday contexts, makes these unique poems a joy to read. Together they build a sort of mythical landscape embracing family and friends, as well as magic and transformations, conjured up in ordinary daily life. They are also well-researched and full of intriguing detail. Places are recognisable, scenes relatable, while also being highly individual, as if the world is being viewed from a different angle.

In the final poem, 'Yew Needle', the last few lines talk of new beginnings:

> Time to slip this choker of aril beads,
> take up a green and dangerous needle
> and stitch yourself a new skin

This is not the end, it implies, the wheel of the year keeps turning.

These are poems strongly rooted in nature, place and family, with an undercurrent of something more pagan: a connection with the rhythm of the seasons, folklore and myth.

All three of these collections explore altered landscapes and how humans as well as animals, adapt to changed conditions. All three in their different ways are remarkable.

About the Author
Sally Baker is a poet, workshop tutor and occasional reviewer. Poems have appeared in *Pennine Platform*, *Propel*, *The North*, *Strix* and the Nine Arches anthology *After Sylvia*. Her pamphlet, *The Sea and The Forest*, was published by The Poetry Business.

KAYLEIGH JAYSHREE

Amelia Loulli, *Slip*, 88pp, £13.00, Cape Poetry
Lucy Mercer, *Emblem*, 108pp, £12.00, Prototype
Emily Berry, *Unexhausted Time*, 88pp, £12.99, Faber & Faber

Described as 'essential' and 'moving', *Slip* is a collection about loss, grief, abortion, fairytales motherhood and blood, lots of blood. Reminiscent of Amy Acre's MOTHERSONG (2023) in its stark look at bodily autonomy and predilection for making the reader uncomfortable and disturbed, Loulli revels in discomfort, fear and angst. *Slip* is split into three parts, 'GENESIS', 'LITTLE RED' and 'RAISING DAUGHTERS' which cover historical ground, folklore, the personal/political. I won't linger on it, but the title is deliberately evocative; the slip of a nightdress, the slipping away of a miscarriage, slipping from one existence to another.

Loulli's poem 'Coming to Terms With Our Abortion in a Tracey Emin Exhibition' in the first section uses language that is reminiscent of Sylvia Plath and the keen eye of a science fiction writer, capturing the everyday horrors a person may face if they have ever lost a baby or had an abortion. The line 'my eyes / the opaque containers   they put the babies in' is an unusual and arresting image. In 'Lady Mary of the Abortion Clinic', Loulli reappropriates Biblical figures. A poignant moment in the poem is the line 'I tell everyone motherhood is a country you can't leave' whilst set in a house party. Loulli imagines Mary aborting Jesus with the line 'the surgeon hovered at her feet   a

The references to motherhood being a country, a border, a prison or place of no return is arresting and tiptoes into intersectionality ...

messenger with a suction tube and the Jesus in her womb vanished without a trace'. It's a strange thing to ask; if the Virgin Mary could have had an abortion, would she? I thought this line of questioning was engaging and one of the boldest poems in *Slip*. The references to motherhood being a country, a border, a prison or place of no return is arresting and tiptoes into intersectionality; the concept that some women are forced into motherhood, into surrogacy or are financially unable to consider an abortion makes the act of abortion a class issue as well as a feminist one. It's these lines of enquiry that I enjoyed most and wish to see more of in Loulli's future work.

Slip's second part covers and reveals different understandings and references the Little Red Riding Hood fairytale. Each poem in the 'LITTLE RED' section is connected by their reference to folklore, I would have liked to see more foregrounding in each poem about the myth and whether the speakers between each poem were connected. The poems in this section are reminiscent of Anne Sexton. Loulli, like Sexton, has a poem titled 'The Abortion'; in Loulli's poem the speaker writes 'I was a wolf / And I lost Little Red / the way a mother loses a child'. In Sexton's poem called 'The Abortion', her speaker says 'up in Pennsylvania, I met a little man, / not Rumpelstiltskin, at all, at all... / he took the fullness that love began.' Loulli's poem about little red riding hood and the big bad wolf is in conversation with Anne Sexton and by extension *Slip* draws on the tradition of female poets writing about child loss and abortion.

'Two Centimetres Dilated' pays attention to the brevity of the line told over a single sentence, a concrete poem where the structure takes the shape of an umbilical cord. The next poem, 'Slip' repeats language from the poem in the previous section 'The Abortion' once again calling the aborted a 'little slip of cells'. 'Slip' was the strongest poem in the collection and the one I found myself connecting to as a reader and reviewer. The lines 'I lean against my bedroom wall listen to the storm / rain soaking the brick staining red / my hands on the inside almost touching almost owing /

the water as it falls' cascaded and were moving. Loulli shows so much potential as a poet especially when she gives space for her images to breathe, and moves away from explaining her speakers' narratives.

Lucy Mercer's collection *Emblem* concerns motherhood, language and the self. I came into reading *Emblem* without an awareness of its formal context. An 'emblem' is a pictorial genre, popular during the 16th and 17th century and splices together images, mottos and short texts. Without knowing this, I read *Emblem* and couldn't get into the collection, the seemingly disparate voices, the impenetrability of the reading. I was confused and frustrated that Mercer didn't give the reader immediacy or an answer. As I read the collection over and over in a brightly-lit spring garden, I started enjoying it. *Emblem* is split into multiple parts: 'Emblem', 'Text & Image', 'The Thing is The Cloud', 'Notation', 'Never Stops Busily Plaiting Ropes From Broom', and 'Emblemata'. In 'Speaking Pictures', the last poem in *Emblem*, the speaker creates parallels between images, words, and speaking, with the line '-some prefer pictures to voices – which is to say they prefer death to life–' which, for me, illuminated the collection as a whole. Mercer and the speakers of her poems seem concerned about death and life and use their voice to reference the strange act of speaking. It's an ambitious book and the strength of *Emblem* itself is using that bold, wide scope in unique and surreal ways. Lucy Mercer resists a neat, wrapped ending, for the benefit of a collection that lends itself to rereads and close attention.

In the first few lines of Mercer's poem 'Single Mother', the speaker declares that:

> The sea dropped its findings or unfastened
> as two brief-lit hard parapets unfastened
> made a wild chronotope out of my body

The 'wild chronotope' Mercer is describing refers to Mikhail Bakhtin's theory of the chronotope, which is a part of narrative theory that refers to or analyses how time and space are used in literature. Put simply, a

Mercer and the speakers of her poems seem concerned about death and life and use their voice to reference the strange act of speaking.

chronotope can refer to how time can be slowed down or sped up in a novel, or in a poem. Mercer interpolates theory and emotion, quite present in the rest of the collection. The speaker's concern and reference to the sea and wildness are fresh and original and are reinforced by later lines where the speaker describes the act of motherhood, or single motherhood as alien or unusual. This struggle with connection or feeling of disorientation or disconnection is acutely seen in the precise choice of language and reference to narrative theory. *Emblem* is focused on abstractions, visual art and the act of knowing/remembering and the inconsistency of being alive, of living. I found myself connecting more to *Emblem* than *Slip* as I found some of the language used in *Slip* to be slightly off-putting, where Loulli's speakers use language deliberately to startle, shock, or alienate the reader. Both poets capture a feeling of discontent, dissociation; whereas Lucy Mercer's speakers in *Emblem* often serve as insignias or emblems themselves for affect or meaning, Loulli's speakers howl, are explicit with their discontent, and wish to project that onto the reader, onto the air.

This chronotopic repetition is seen in *Emblem* in the poem 'Minutes of Hexogram 17', as Mercer plays with ideas of space, time and how they are represented in written and visual form. The poem splits into three stanzas that repeat and remix the language of the previous in a carnival-esque style to describe a picture of the evening: 'Follow me outside the open gate / the sky is sleeping fringed and pink.' The stanzas, as a whole act as a concrete poem taking the shape of a garden fence. The rhythm and meter of 'Minutes of Hexogram 17' creating a disturbed, distrusting emotion in the reader, particularly when the poem is read aloud. Mercer's trust in her work and the reader makes her collection more enjoyable, complex, and multi-faceted. Lucy Mercer's skill as a poet lies in her giving the space between images and meaning, making her poetry a more sensory and challenging experience, going beyond the familiar.

Emily Berry's *Unexhausted Time* is less linear than her previous collection, *Stranger, Baby* and goes into the surreal in a similar vein to Lydia Davis and Lorrie Moore. In her poem, 'Empty', Berry's speaker says, 'I thought of my own womb hanging empty inside me and was pierced with joy' using words like 'pierced' and 'empty' which usually are there to give shock value, but in the context of the poem, the speaker is pleased with their empty womb, rather than mournful. Emily Berry's writing can at times both feel ghostly and cacophonous and has inspired a new generation of poets, from the brilliant New Poets Prize winner Chloe Elliot's micro chapbook DREAMSIMULATION to Tom Bailey's Poetry London Prize winning pamphlet 'Do Not Touch or Feed the Horses'. In her poem 'Empty' Berry leaves the subtext to the reader's imagination, instead painting the space between the speaker and their friend as complicated, painful, joyous. Pregnancy, fear, motherhood, violence are entwined into one where the speaker feels relief at their own empty womb. *Unexhausted Time* by Emily Berry is chronotopic in a similar way to *Slip* and *Emblem;* where *Slip* demonstrates a pierced, stretched out time where myths can parallel and contradict, *Emblem* shows a repeated jaunt in the garden that warps into a funhouse mirror and *Unexhausted Time* continually stretches out loss to avoid the exhaustion of grief.

In another poem, '(The story is a leaf)', there's a brilliant group of lines:

Bad?
The star was festering. Coldness around
all of my love. There was a woman
who stopped me in the street to shout
in my face about the violence she'd seen
in me.

Berry's sense of rhythm, sound and line breaks add to the distanced and semi-ironic humour displayed in *Unexhausted Time*, ballooning up emotions and watching them drift, pop, bloat. I like how Berry resists the expected yet uses ordinary situations and dials them up to eleven. Throughout *Unexhausted Time* Berry doesn't rely on a reader's familiarity with situations

Emily Berry's writing can at times both feel ghostly and cacophonous and has inspired a new generation of poets ...

and events, in 'Opinion' and 'Therapy', two mundane situations, bumping into your therapist and having a group therapy session. At first, I found 'Opinion' to be quite jarring. Surely the speaker is behaving unrealistically? Why wouldn't they just react like a normal person? After discussing this poem with other people and hearing their reactions, I've come to realise there's a lot of fear of vulnerability in *Unexhausted Time*: fear of opening up, of your cold love being exposed, being afraid of someone knowing how you feel, even if it's just about your shoes, even if it's a person who is supposed to make you feel safe. Emily Berry describes therapeutic disclosure in 'Therapy' as troubling self-expression, which is a neat way to think about *Unexhausted Time*: modes of the self, of expression and how that can be flipped, warped or problematised.

About the Author

Kayleigh Jayshree is a poet and critic. Her reviews have been published by *PN Review*, *Poetry Book Society* and *Ink Sweat & Tears*. Her poems have been published by *Butcher's Dog* and Young Poets Network. Her debut pamphlet is forthcoming with fourteenpoems.

Kayleigh was a digital poet in residence with the Poetry Business https://poetrybusiness.co.uk/2023/07/12/karishma-sangtani-in-conversation-with-kayleigh-jayshree/

INDEX OF POETS AND POEMS

ISOBEL DIXON
  Thoughts on the 22:20 Avanti West Coast Train to London Euston 5

DAVID CONSTANTINE
  Transit of the bin-men 6
  Lifeline 6
  Aurelia in hiding 7
  Speech Day 7

DAVID TAIT
  Faerie 8
  Leighton Moss 8
  Between Storms 9

JAMES BRADLEY
  Hoopoe 9

NIAMH TWOMEY
  Herb 10
  Follow Me 10
  At Arrivals 11

JACKIE WILLS
  The Night Before I Turn 70 11

PENELOPE SHUTTLE
  hip hip hooray 12
  Arwyn Place 28 January 2025 12

ROY MARSHALL
  Lull 13
  A Fire 13

BRENDAN CLEARY
  Reservoir1 4
  Classics 14

PHILIP RUSH
  Solidarity and Peace 15

MARTIN HAYDEN
  An incomplete, unrhymed sonnet, in memory of Peter Abbs, poet and educationalist 16

JENNY McROBERT
  First Gooseberry 16

MARTYN CRUCEFIX
  Scream 17
  Things Newborn 17

RAMONA HERDMAN
  Every medical appointment is like a job interview 18

  Conditional 18
  Lemons 18
  Promise 19

HOWARD WRIGHT
  Transfigured 19

LAUREN CAMP
  One to Borrow Trouble 20
  Drop Me to My Knees 20

JOHN LYNCH
  Antarctica 21
  Reading Week 21

JUNE CREBBIN
  Encounter 22
  alone in the house 22
  For Zoe 23

ELIZABETH CHADWICK
  English Teacher Blues 23

PAULINE PLUMMER
  Corkscrew 24

JACCI BULMAN
  Altocumulus clouds 24

JOHN GOODBY
  Mr Fisher Sits In 25

ORLAGH O'FARRELL
  Relation 26
  Uncle Dessie 26

MAITREYABANDHU
  Beaudesert and Swancroft 27

TIM DOOLEY
  Waking, 27

SUE RILEY
  Waking to Oranges 28
  Frog Morning 28

JULIE LUMSDEN
  Welcome to Nottingham 29

LORRAINE Mc ARDLE
  Princess Magic Touch™ Presumed Dead 29

IAN POPLE
  Even the dock 30

MAGGIE REED
  these bright moments 30

NIA BROOMHALL
  On Sitting 31
  Horses 31

JEAN STEVENS
  Hooves 32
  Bucket List 32

FOKKINA McDONNELL
  Landscape with a footbridge 33
  Take my advice, 33

BARBARA MARSH
  Wild horses 34
  18th arrondissement 34
  Almost approaching the station 35

TERRY QUINN
  On Bare Lane Station 35

PAUL MILLS
  Pastoral 36

DAVID UNDERDOWN
  My street 37
  The Homecoming 37

MEG COX
  Not Quite 38
  Despite 38

MIKE DI PLACIDO
  Another poem about David Hockney 39
  Vertiginous at Opening Time 39

JOHN LANCASTER
  An Attendance Officer Calls 40
  Uncredited 41

STEPHEN PAYNE
  Puddings 42

PAM THOMPSON
  To Brighton Pier 42

ROBERT ETTY
  Wednesday 43

ROBERT HAMBERGER
  Rich Man Poor Man 43

VASILIKI ALBEDO
  Schnapps 44
  Pamplona 44

CHRISTY KU
  Homecoming 45

LIZ BYRNE
    Headless 45
CHARLOTTE WETTON
    Bureau de Change 46
ROD WHITWORTH
    Alternative medicine 47
    Calan the light-carrier 47
MARY NOONAN
    Weather 48
    At the Bassins de Lumières 48
SIÚN CARDEN
    Scale Model 49
MICHAEL HENRY
    Making Nice 49
LYDIA HARRIS
    translating the prone woman 50
JENNY KING
    Woman with two greyhounds 52
JON MILLER
    Transient 53
    Old Flame 53
BEN McGUIRE
    What I Still Know About Procida 54
    The Way the Weeks Away Came Back 54
JIM McELROY
    Michael, Do You Ever Regret 55
AMY DUGMORE
    Zuihitsu on the joys of small breasts 56
    Hero 57
EILIS STANLEY
    Cow day 57
ROSIE HADDEN
    A night out in Tyrone circa April 1981 58
JEANETTE BURTON
    Outstanding 59
LYDIA MACPHERSON
    Franconia Notch 60
    Roman Coin Found at Top Withens 61
    Exhibit 61
GRAHAM MORT
    Fever 62
    Insomnia 62

REBECCA ALTHAUS
    I Can't Write About Beauty 63
    In a Field at Midsummer 63
CLIFF YATES
    Bus to Cirencester 64
    Three Dog Night 64
    Bottle 65
LINDA FORD
    Renaissance 65
ANGELA NEENAN
    First symptoms 66
MARION NEW
    Green 66
MATTHEW PAUL
    Green Tomato Chutney 67
    To Me, to You 67
MICHAEL LASKEY
    Firelighters 80
    The Clothes-peg 80
    Bike 81
    Weighing the Present 81
    Nightingales 82
    Between Two Lit Rooms 82
    Between Ourselves 83
    The Last Swim 84
    One Job of Mine 84
JAYANT KASHYAP
    Notes on Burials 86
    On the finding of a body, said to be
    the result of a drug overdose 87
    Dream Sequence 87
CIA MANGAT
    inventory of aunties 88
    sometimes I wonder if my ma is right & I do
    actually fancy boys 89
ZELDA CAHILL-PATTEN
    Pelias 91
    Redwood After Wildfire 91
CHARLIE JOLLEY
    Sid Vicious Walks Alone on Brooklyn
    Bridge, 1978 92
    Tomorrowland 92

CAROLINE BRACKEN
    Black Coat 94
    The Blues 95
    Fabric 95
JEN FEROZE
    I invite my grown-up daughter round
    for dinner 96
    The four of us in August 97
    Grief: A Primer 97
DALE BOOTON
    Mocks 99
    Beyond 99
KATE RUTTER
    Through All This 100
    Cable Car 100
JAMES APPLEBY
    Whale at distance 101
    Given a night of ice 101
GER DUFFY
    Testimony of Soap 102
    Hotpants 102
DERVAL TUBRIDY
    Late 103
    Window 103
NIGEL PANTLING
    Pit Stop 105
    A String of Pearls 105
    Witness Statement 106
    Looking for Tigers 106
    An Inspector Calls 107
    Bosra 107
DEAN PARKIN
    Wallpaper 108
    Norwich Keeper 109
    Removal Men Discuss My Boxes of Books 109
BLIND CRITICISM POET
    The Bomber 110